FANGS and FLAWS

FangGrr Adventures

by Jenny Doh

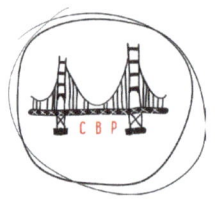

Crescendoh Bridge Press
www.crescendoh.com

Crescendoh Bridge Press
www.crescendoh.com

Doh, Jenny
Fangs and Flaws: FangGrrr Adventures

First Edition

Packaged by Crescendoh Bridge Press
Text and Illustrations © 2014, Jenny Doh

For the FangGrrrs and Lions
within us all.

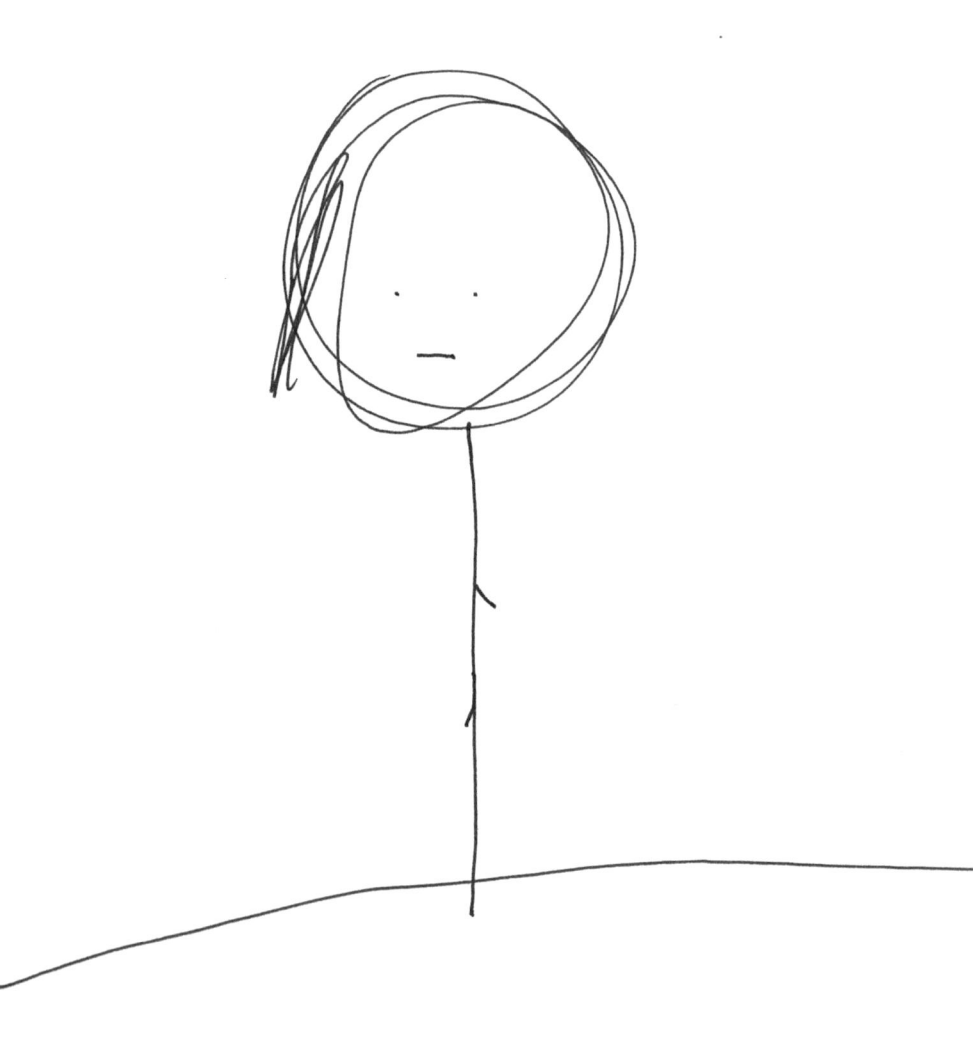

Her mom left.

Then her dad.

And she was sad.

She pretended not
to be sad.

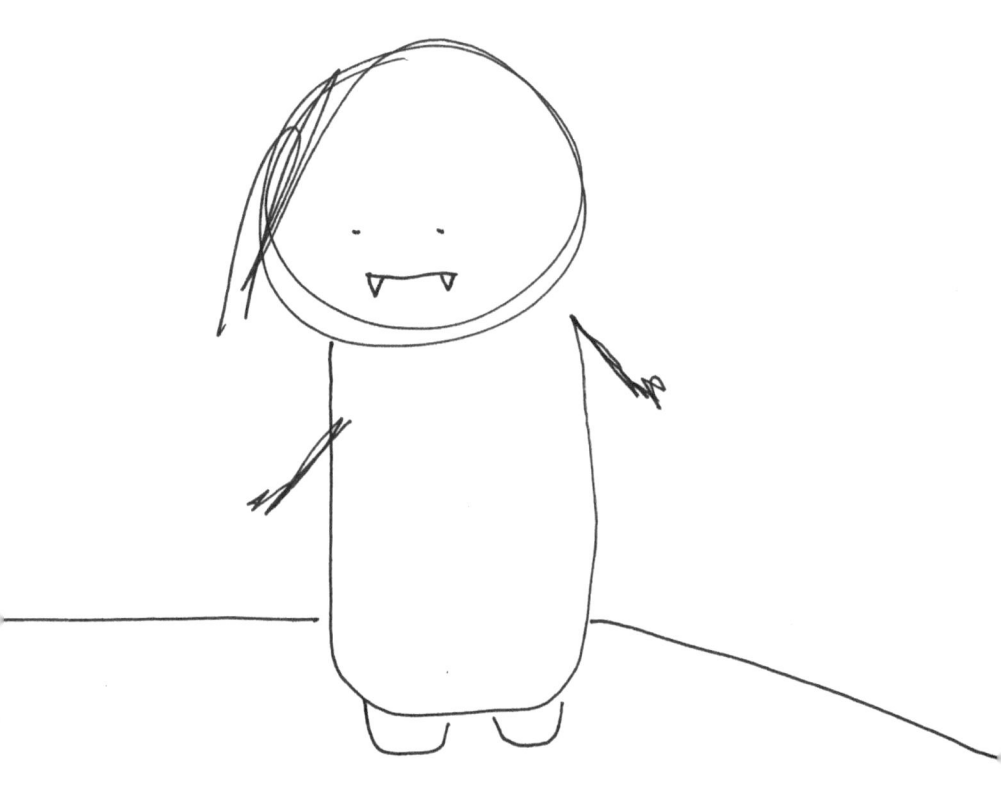

And grew fangs instead.

One day fang girl

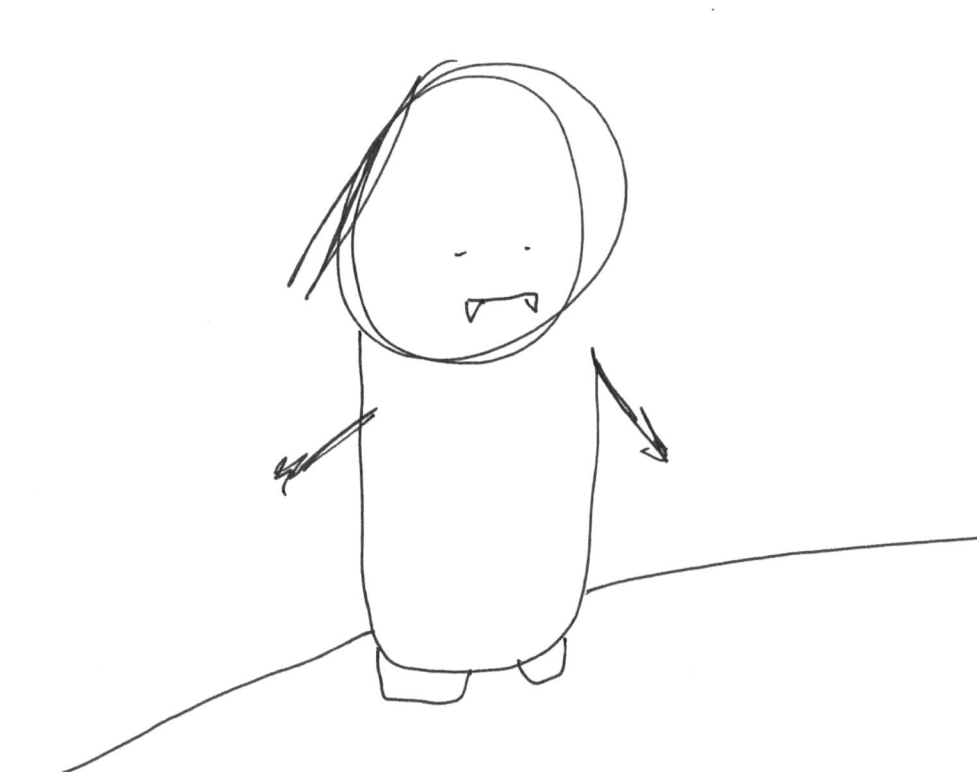

met Lion.

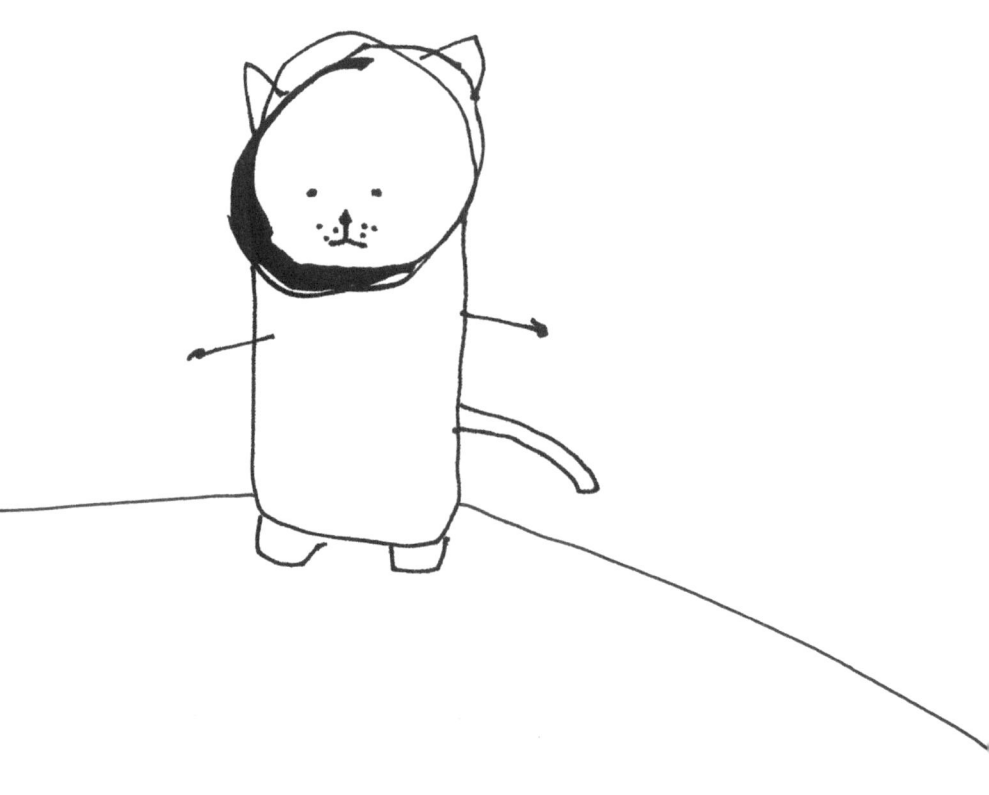

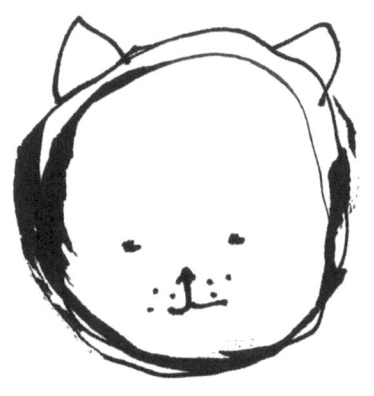

Lion was kind and liked to
play and have fun.
"Let's play, FangGrrr!"
said Lion.

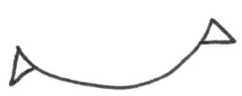

FangGrrr liked being called that.

Being called FangGrrr, that is.

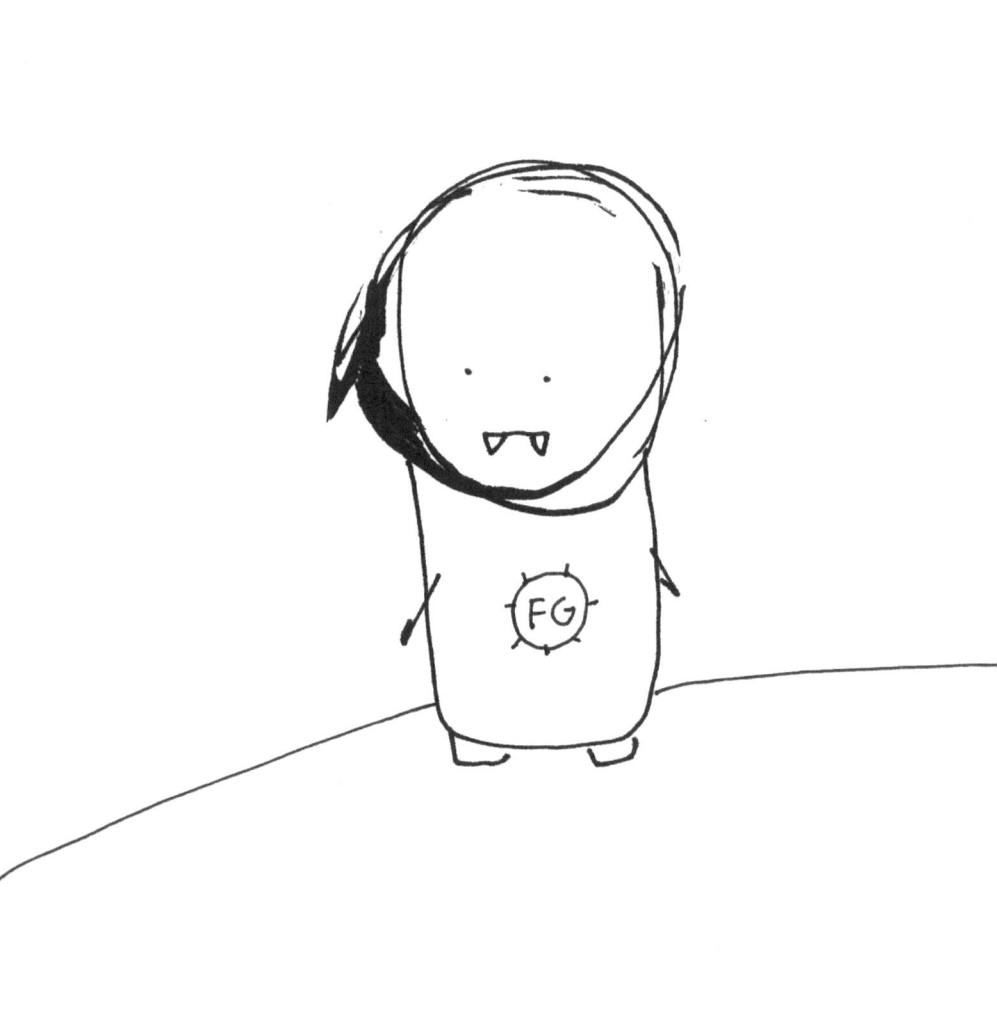

"But Lion,

i don't know

how to play,"

said FangGrr.

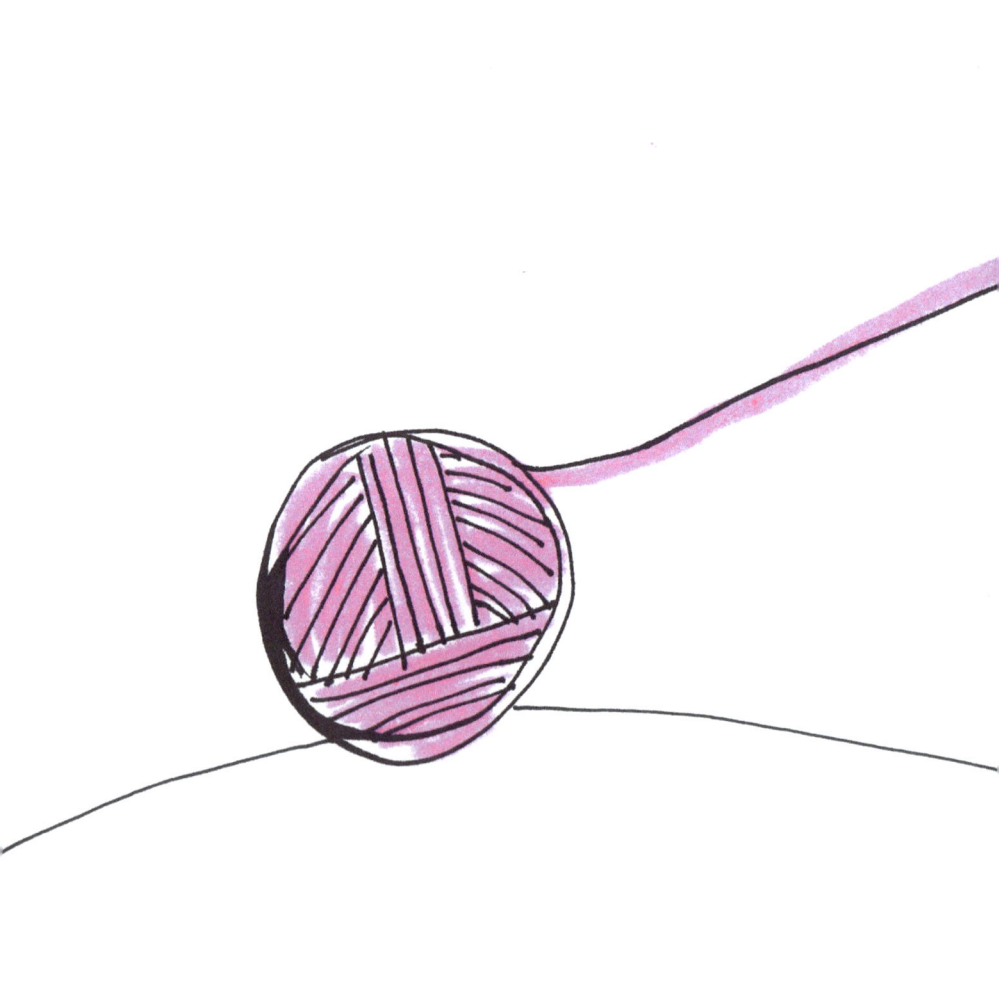

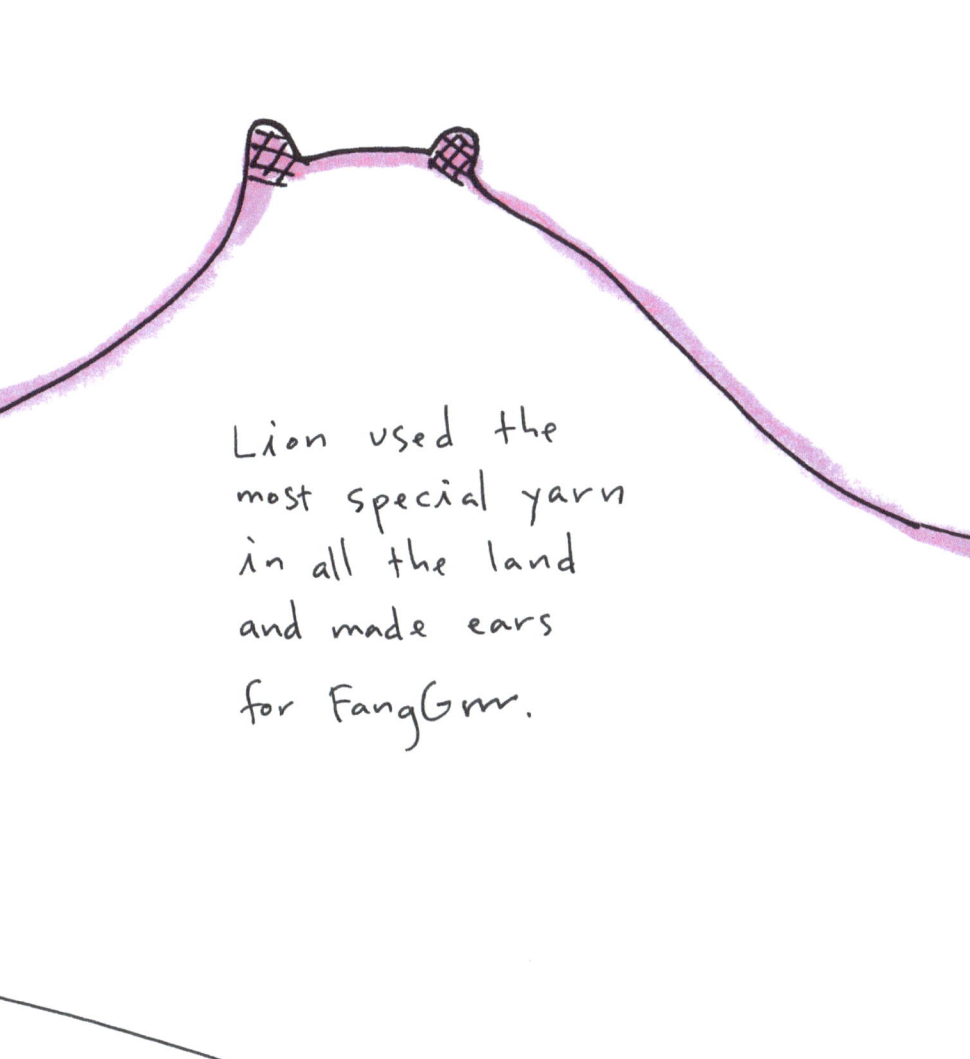

Lion used the most special yarn in all the land and made ears for FangGrr.

The yarn was pink,

of course.

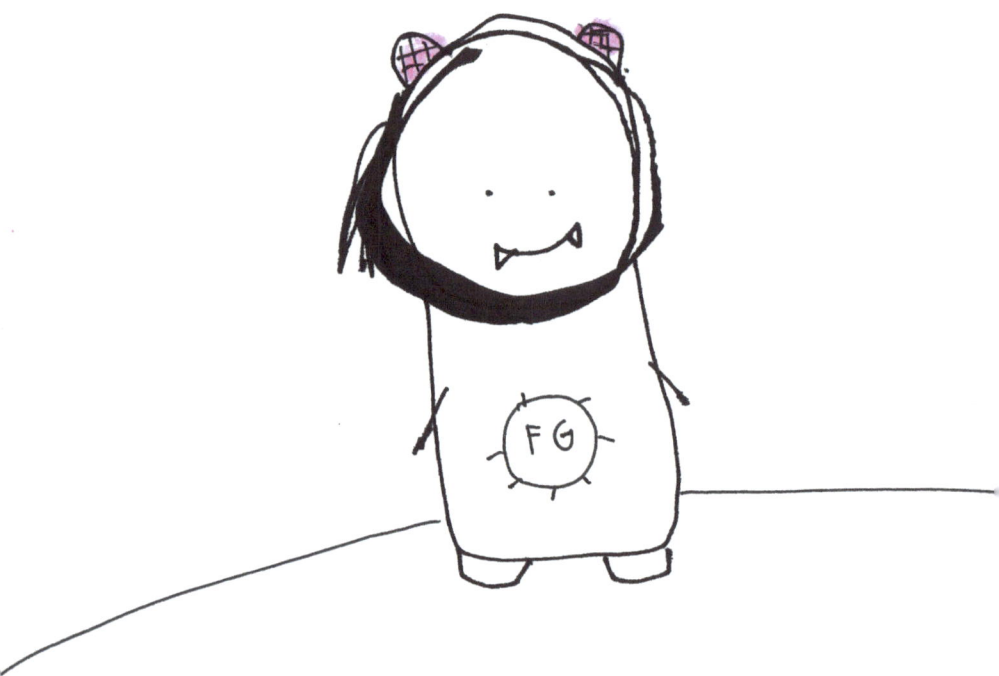

FangGrrr loved the ears.

Actually, FangGirr ruved them.

They made FangGrrr feel special.

With ears on, arms raised,
eyes closed, and Butterfly
aflutter, FangGrrr made
a wish.

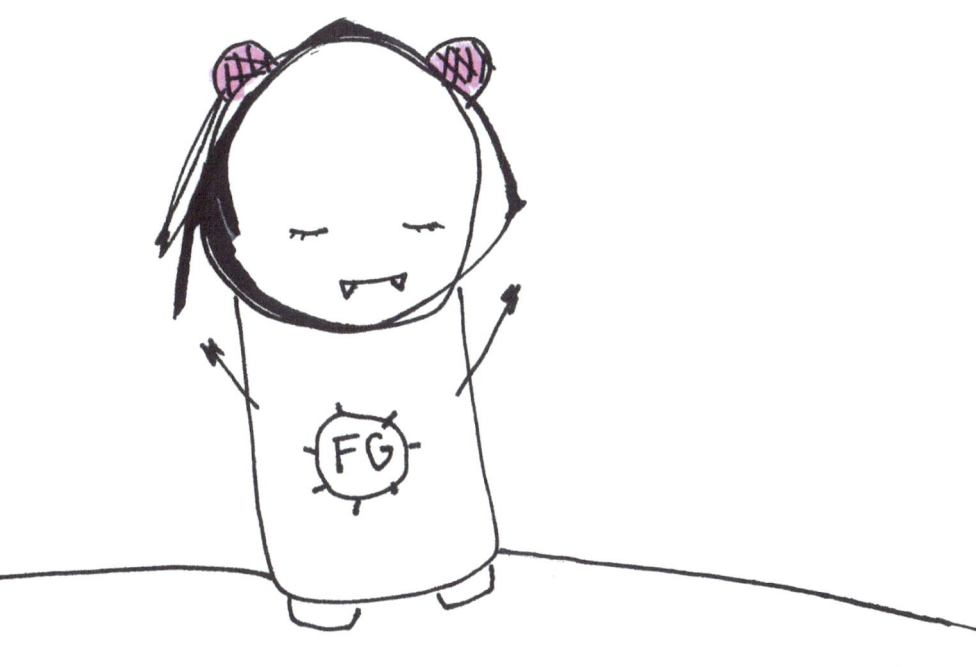

"i wish i could play,"
said FangGrr.

And with that,
FangGrrr and Lion
PLAYED.

They played ball.

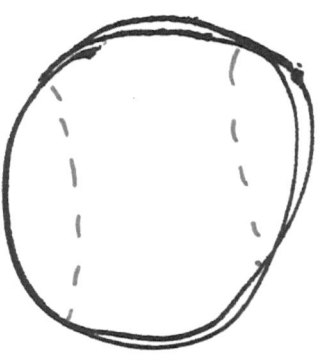

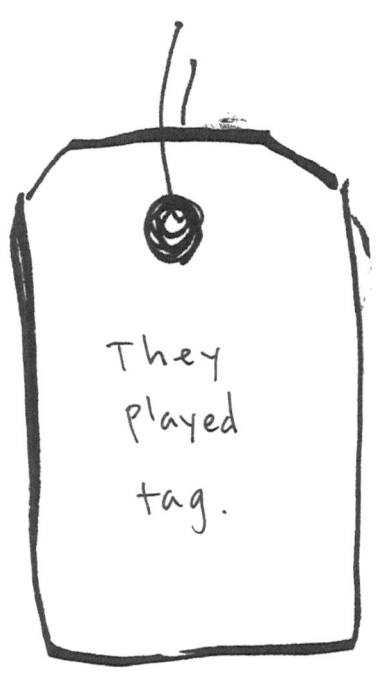

They played tag.

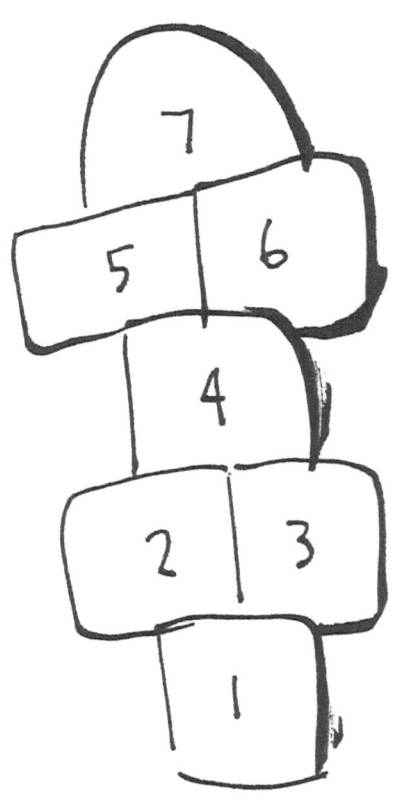

They played hopscotch.

They LAUGHED
while they played.
Until their bellies hurt,
they laughed. (In a good way.)

Sometimes, they took
a break from all
the playing.

to drink chocolate milk.

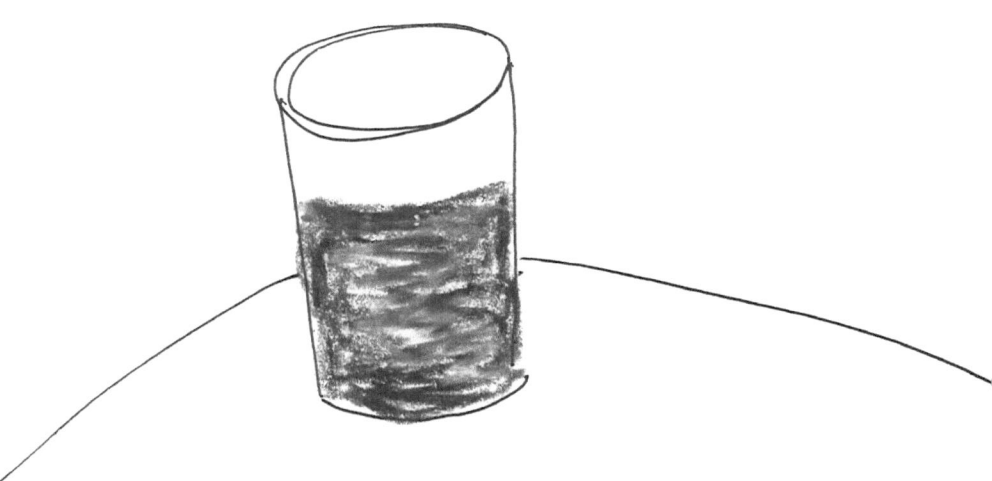

When they started to play after drinking the chocolate milk, they could hear it swish around in their bellies.

Especially during hopscotch.

This made FangGirr
and Lion laugh even more.

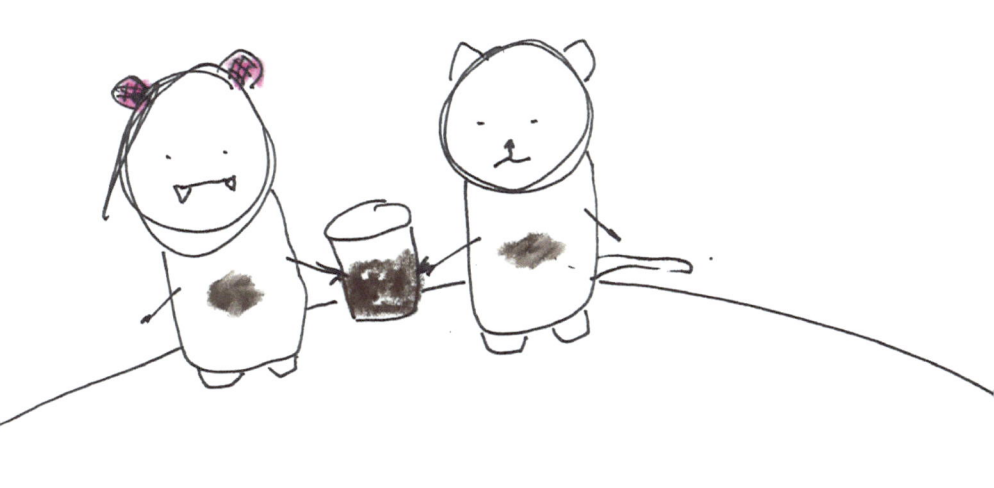

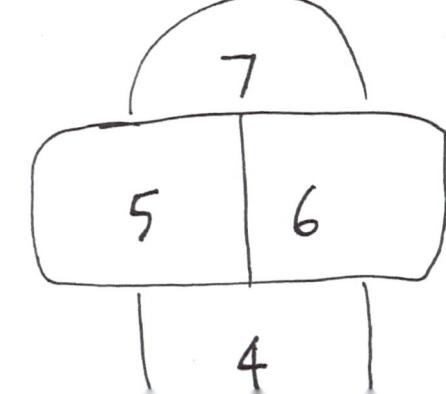

FangGurr was

HAPPY.

(By the way, this is not
the end of this story.)

Not yet.

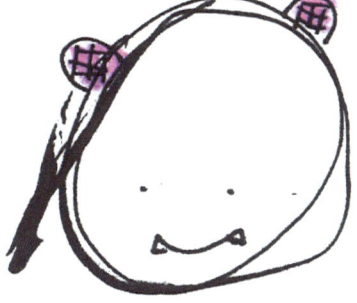

Lion loved Fangbrr.

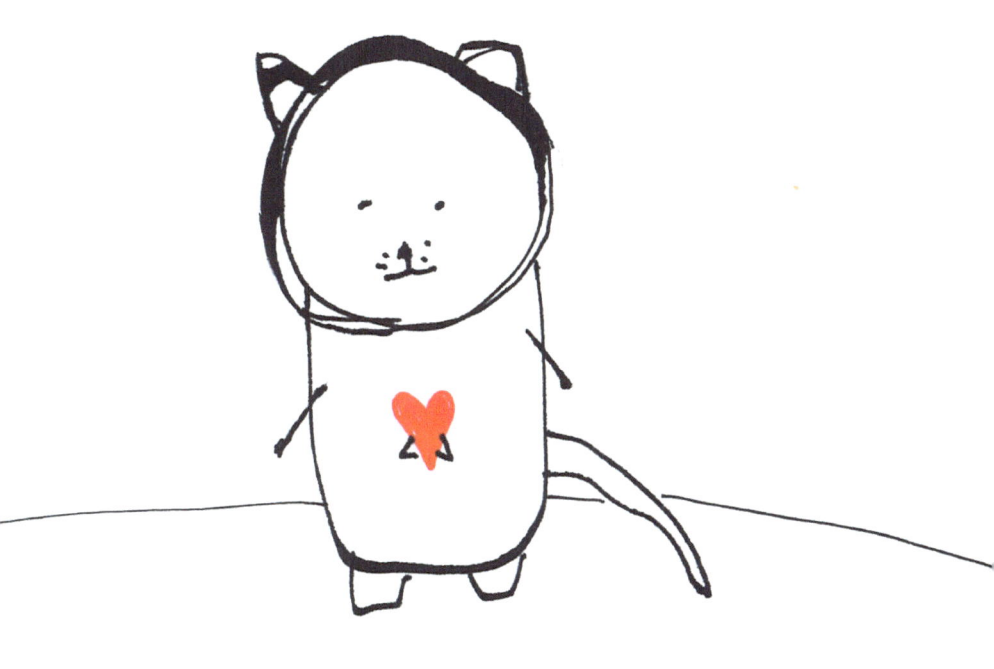

Without conditions.

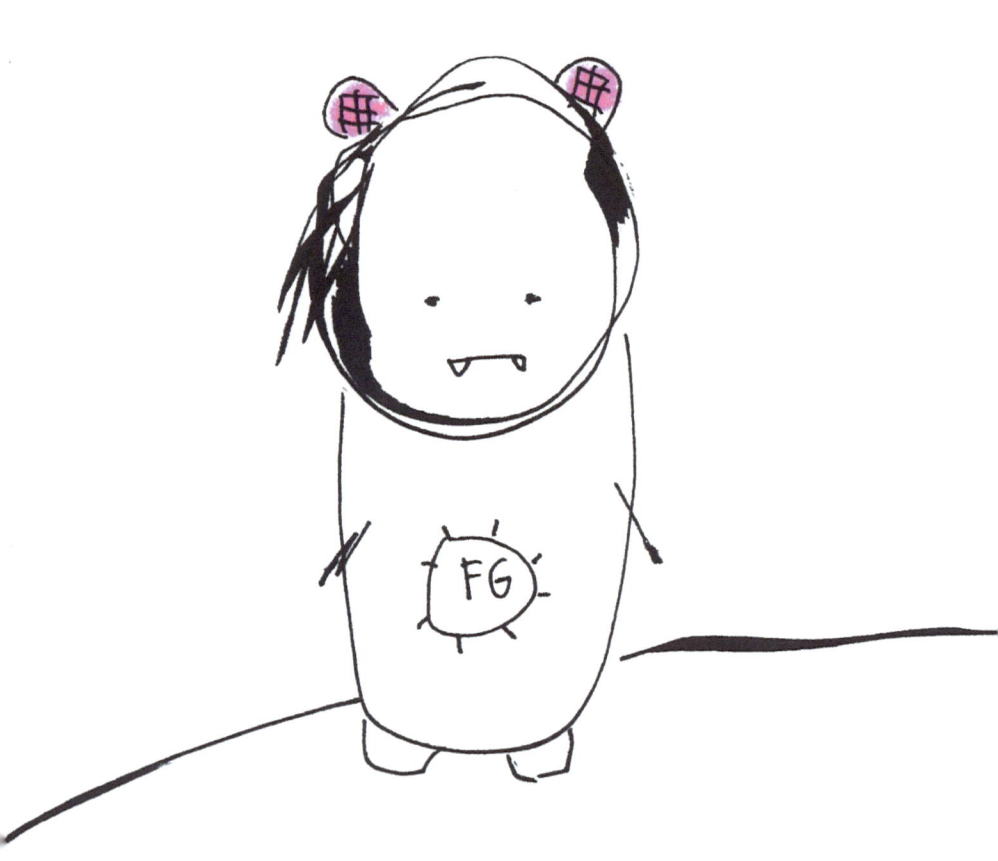

Snake slithered in. "Lion does not love you. You should hurt Lion before Lion hurts you. Before Lion leaves you too," said Snake.

"Sssss...."

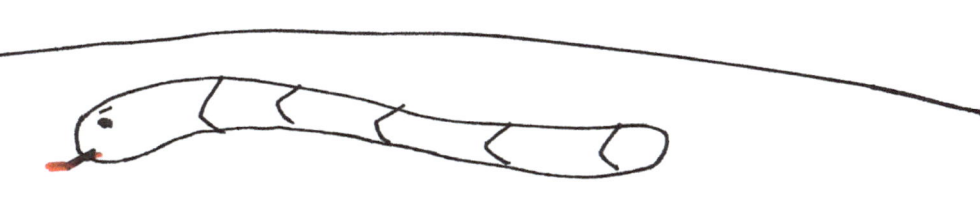

FangGrrr believed Snake.

"i have many voids and flaws.
i have fangs. i am not
lovable. Lion is bound to
leave me too," thought FangGrrr.
With profound sadness,
FangGrrr wept.

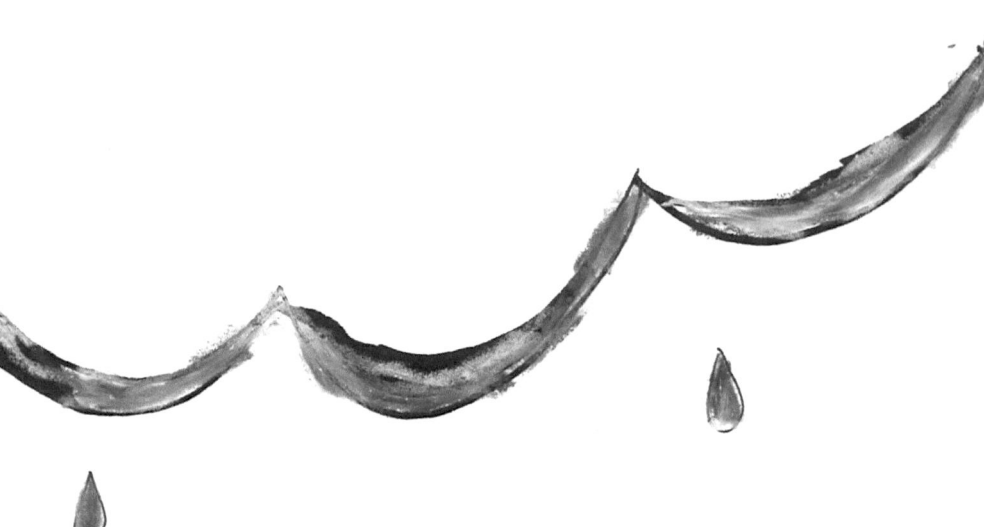

FangGmr's sadness was so intense
that the entire land felt it.

Sun said "auf wiedersehen" as
Clouds rolled in.

For what felt like forever,
Clouds dropped two million
chocolate-milky tear-rain drops
everywhere.

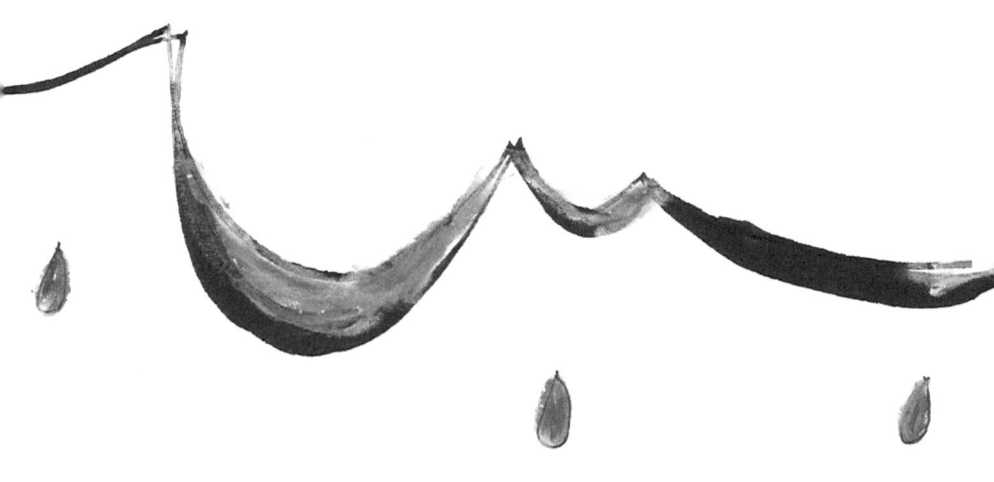

(it may have been three million,
  actually.)

Drops came down
hard,
fast,
and without pause.

Everything and everyone got
drenched in melancholy.

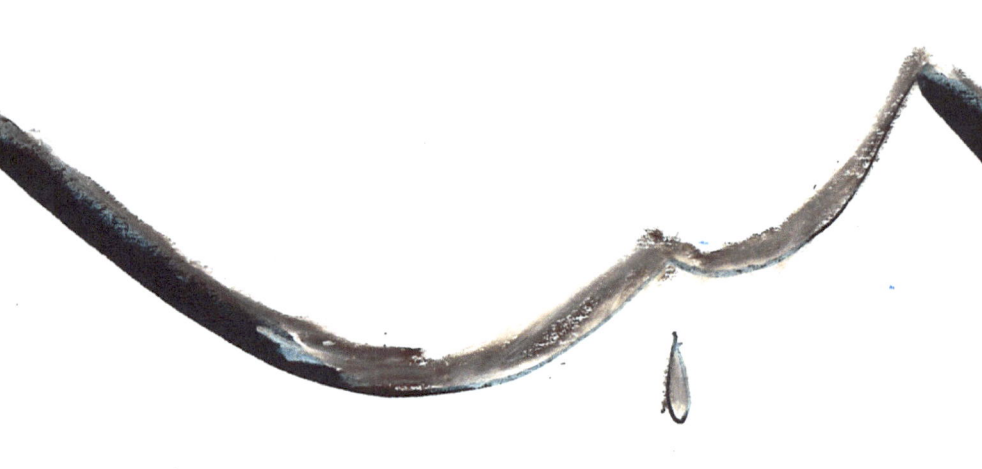

"Stop crying and go hurt
Lion," said Snake to FangGurr.

"And leave your ears here
with me. For ssssafe
keeping."

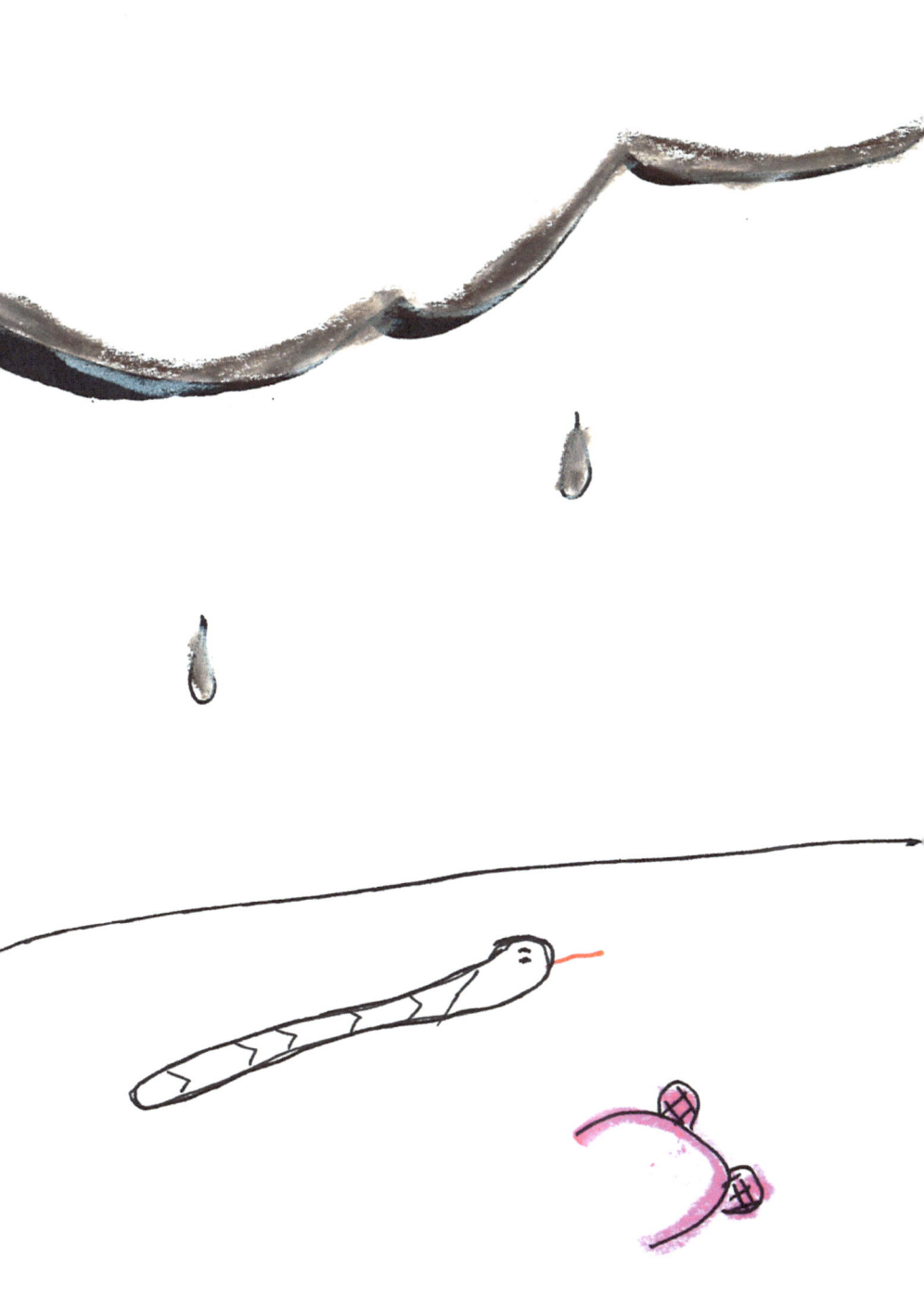

" i dont like you Lion," said FangGrrr. And then FangGrrr punched Lion in the face. Hard.

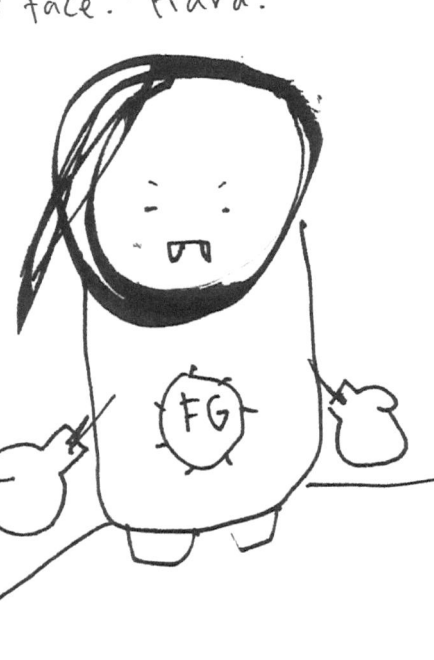

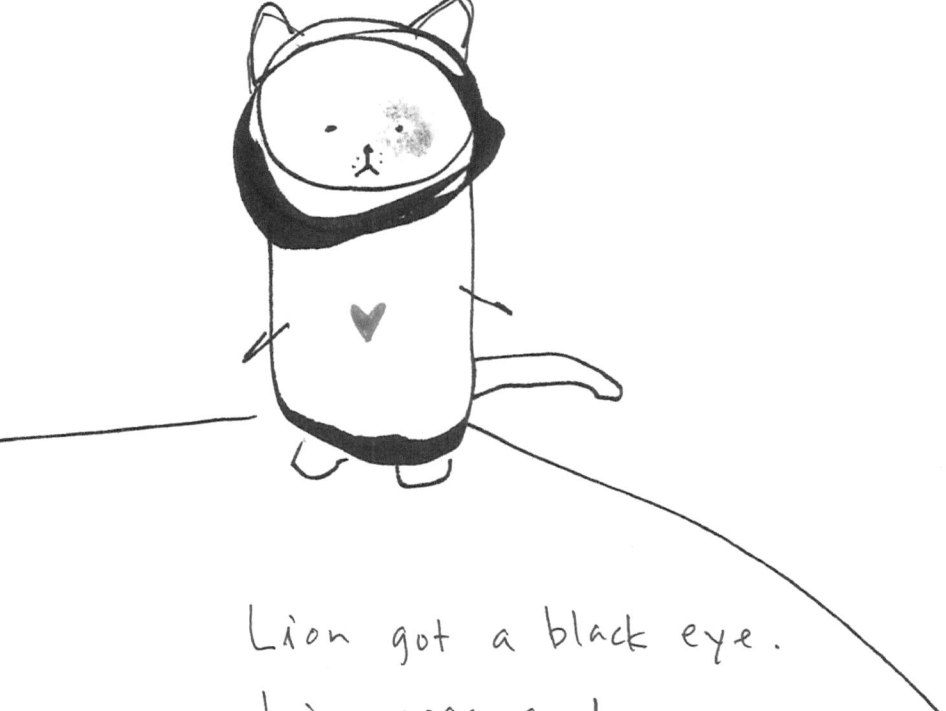

Lion got a black eye.
Lion was sad.

"You need to hurt Lion more sssseveeeerely," said Snake to FangGrrr.

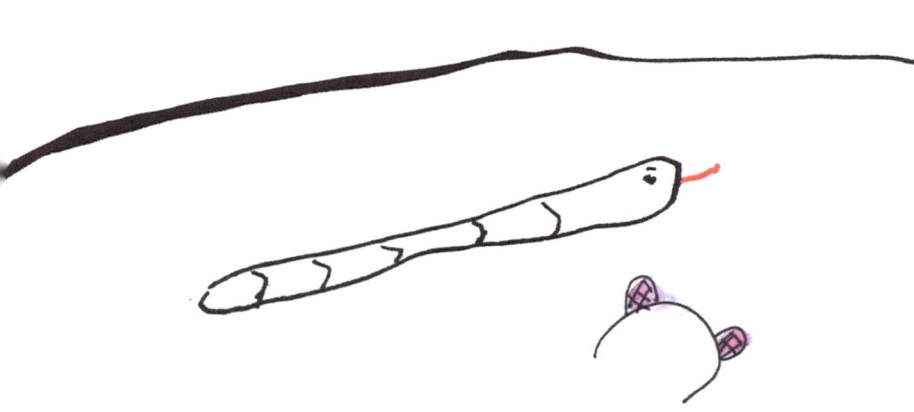

"Take this bow and arrow
and shoot Lion in the
heart."

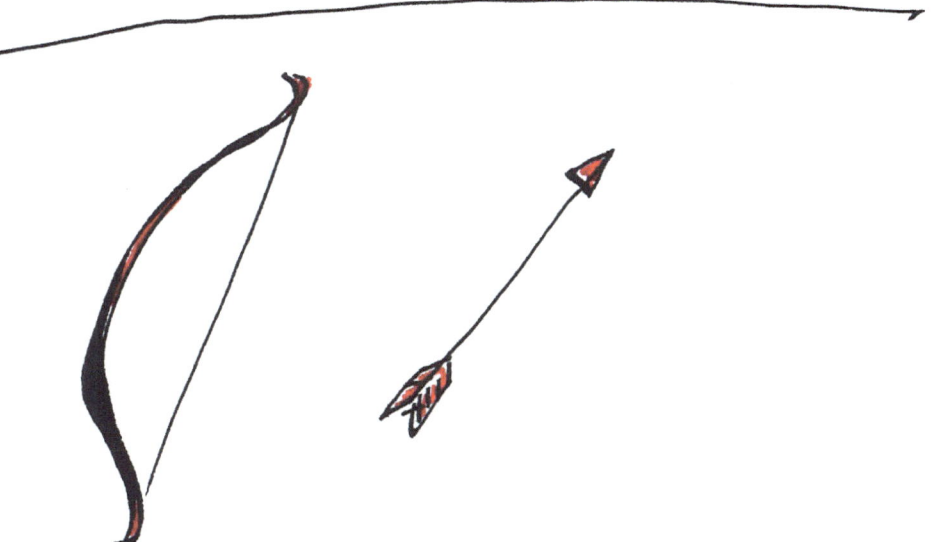

Meanwhile ....
Snake put the ears on.

Snake first wished for lots
of money. Then lots of
power. Then lots of fame.

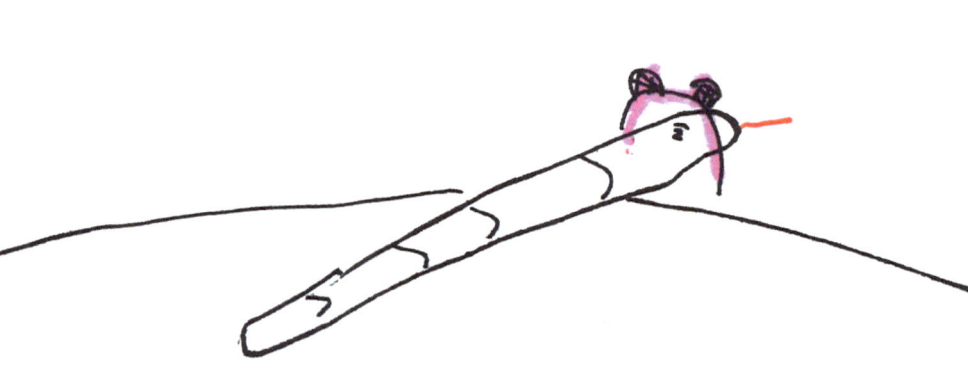

"Those wishes will never come true with those ears," said Butterfly.

"Then what kinds of wishes will come true?" asked Snake.

"Sincere ones made with a pure heart," said Butterfly.

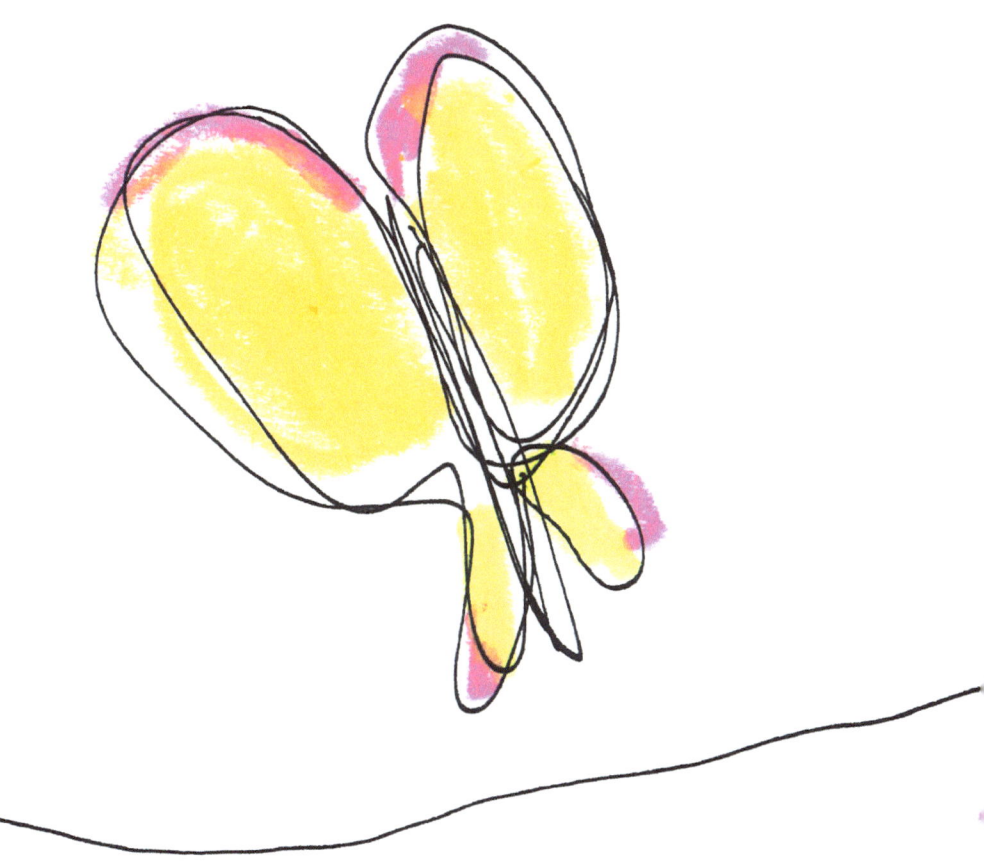

"Where can i find sincerity and a pure heart?" asked Snake.

"Within," said Butterfly, and flew away.

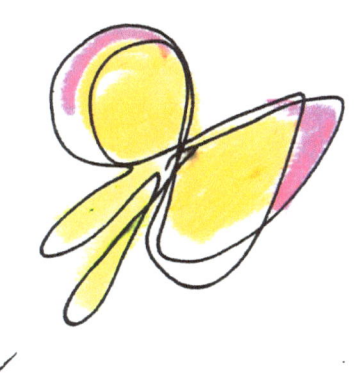

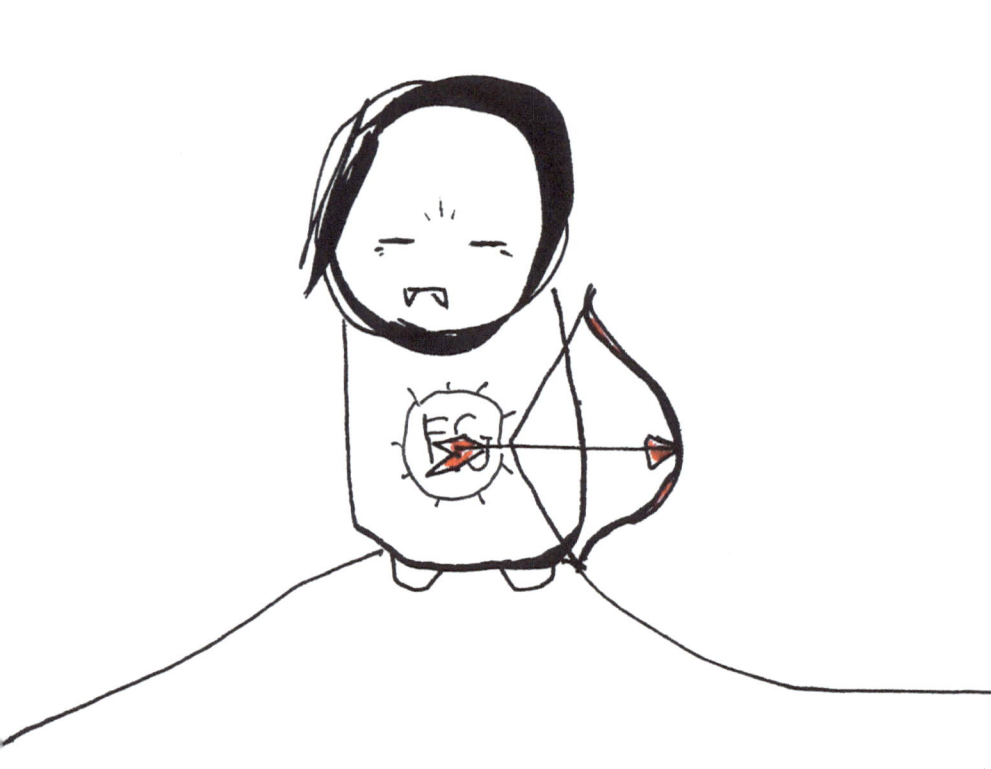

FangGrr drew the bow and arrow and aimed precisely at Lion's heart.

FangGrr released the arrow
and it impaled Lion's heart.

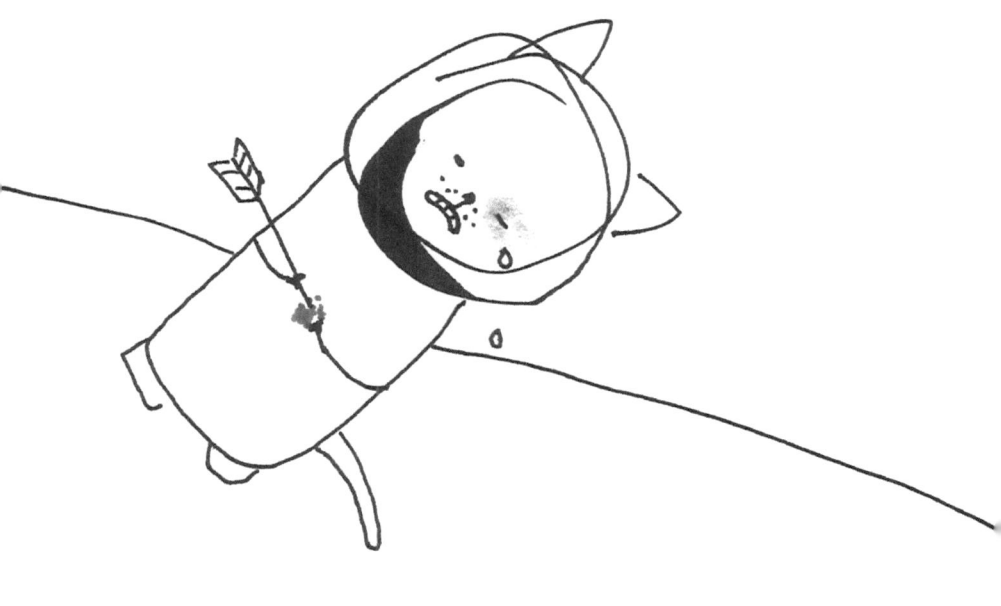

Lion fell to the ground.

"Why have you done this,
FangGrrr?" wept Lion in

sorrow and pain.

"i don't understand."

Remorse filled FangGrrr's heart.

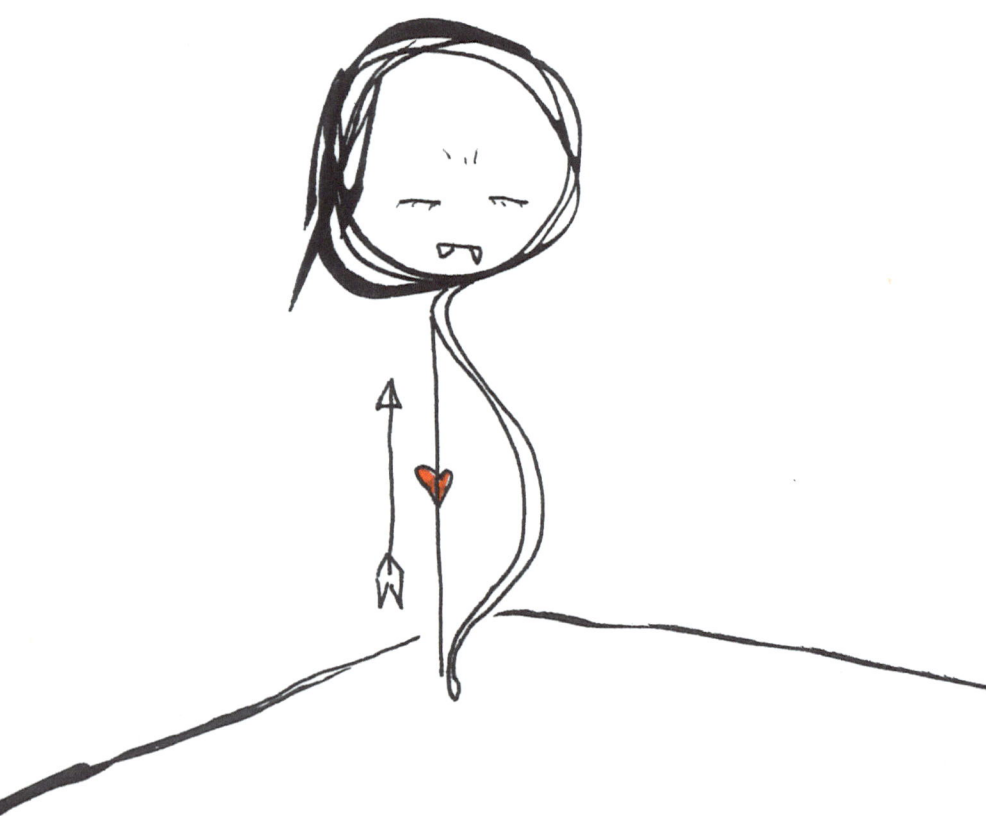

"What have i done?"
FangGur asked.

"I am Sorry Lion.
Forgive me."

FangGrrr pulled the bloody arrow
out of Lion's chest. Lion's chest
kept bleeding.

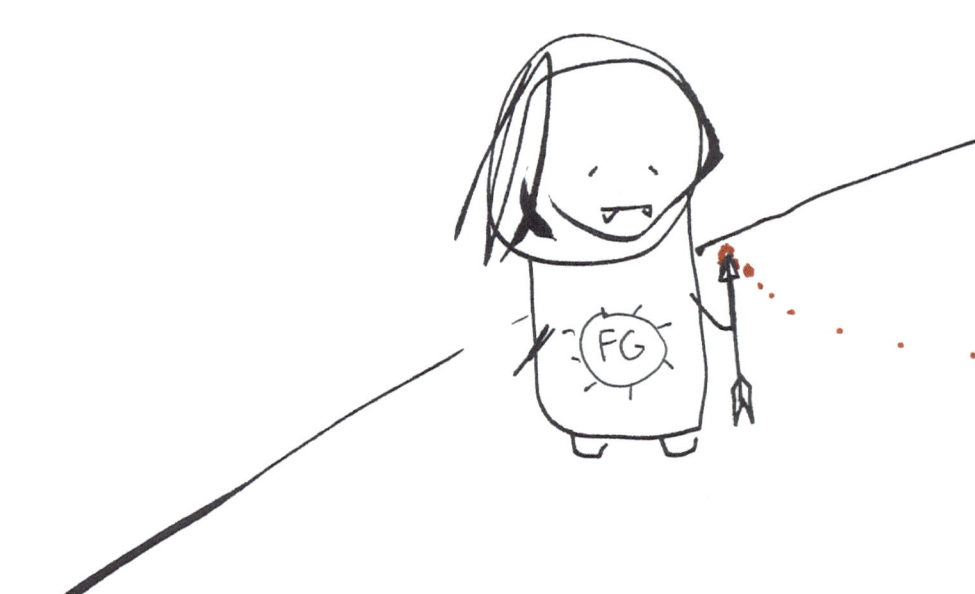

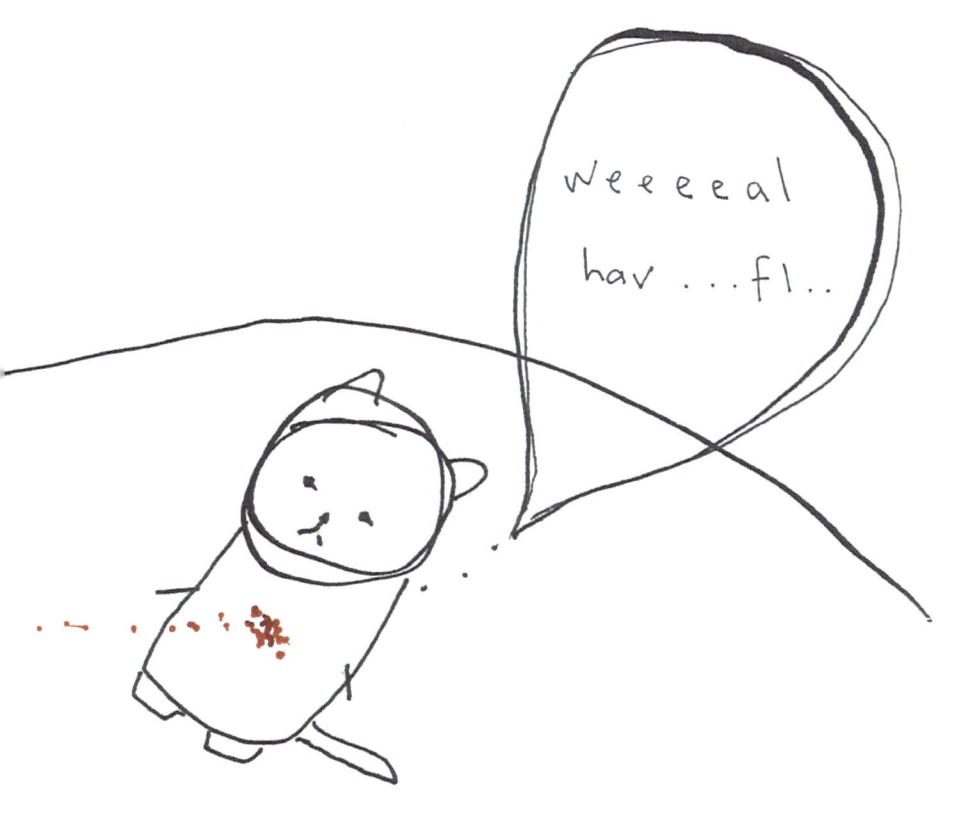

Sounds came out of Lion
that didn't make sense, like
hallucinations before death.

FangGrrr didn't know what
to do.

Hopelessness and shame
flooded into FangGmr's
heart to congregate with
Remorse.

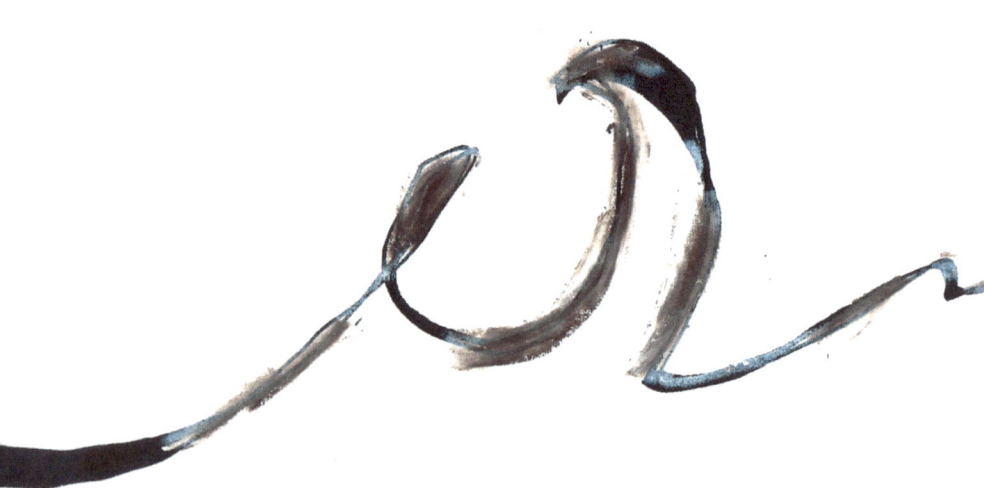

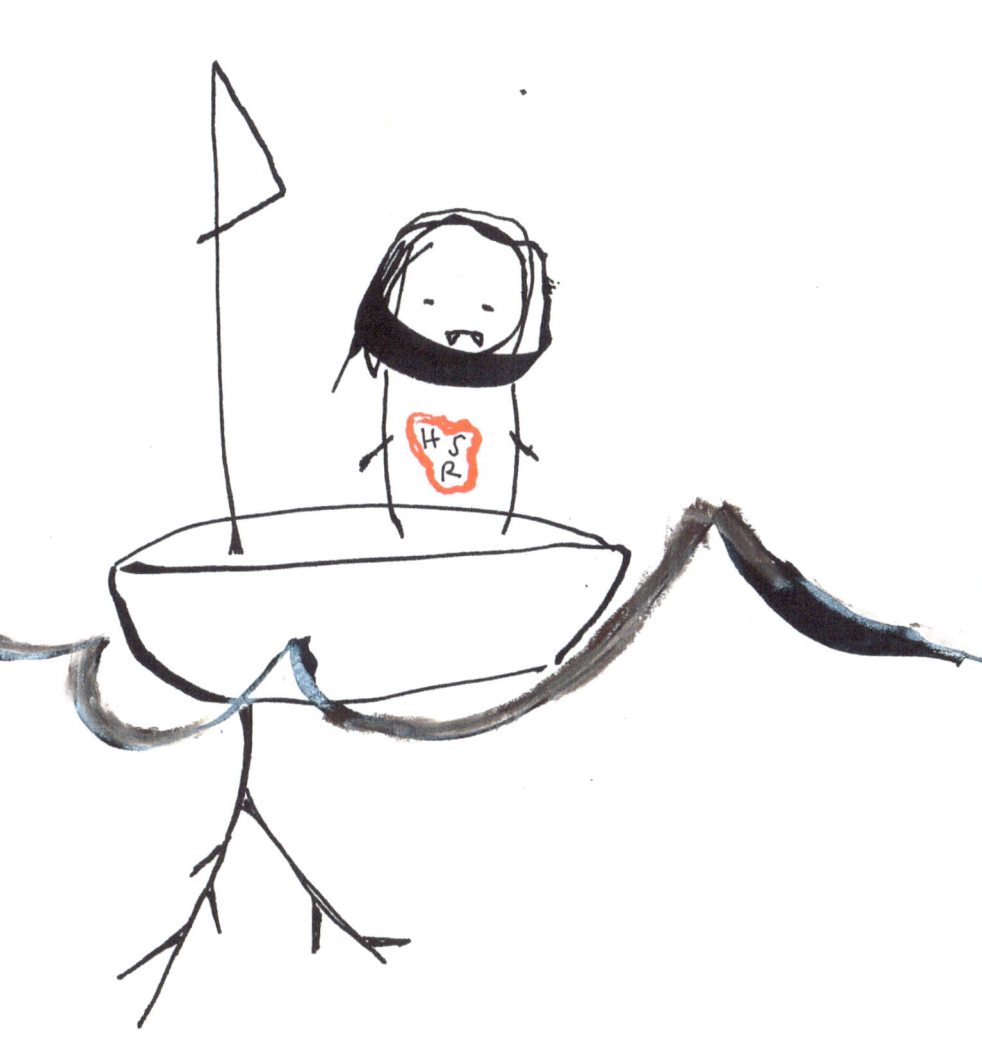

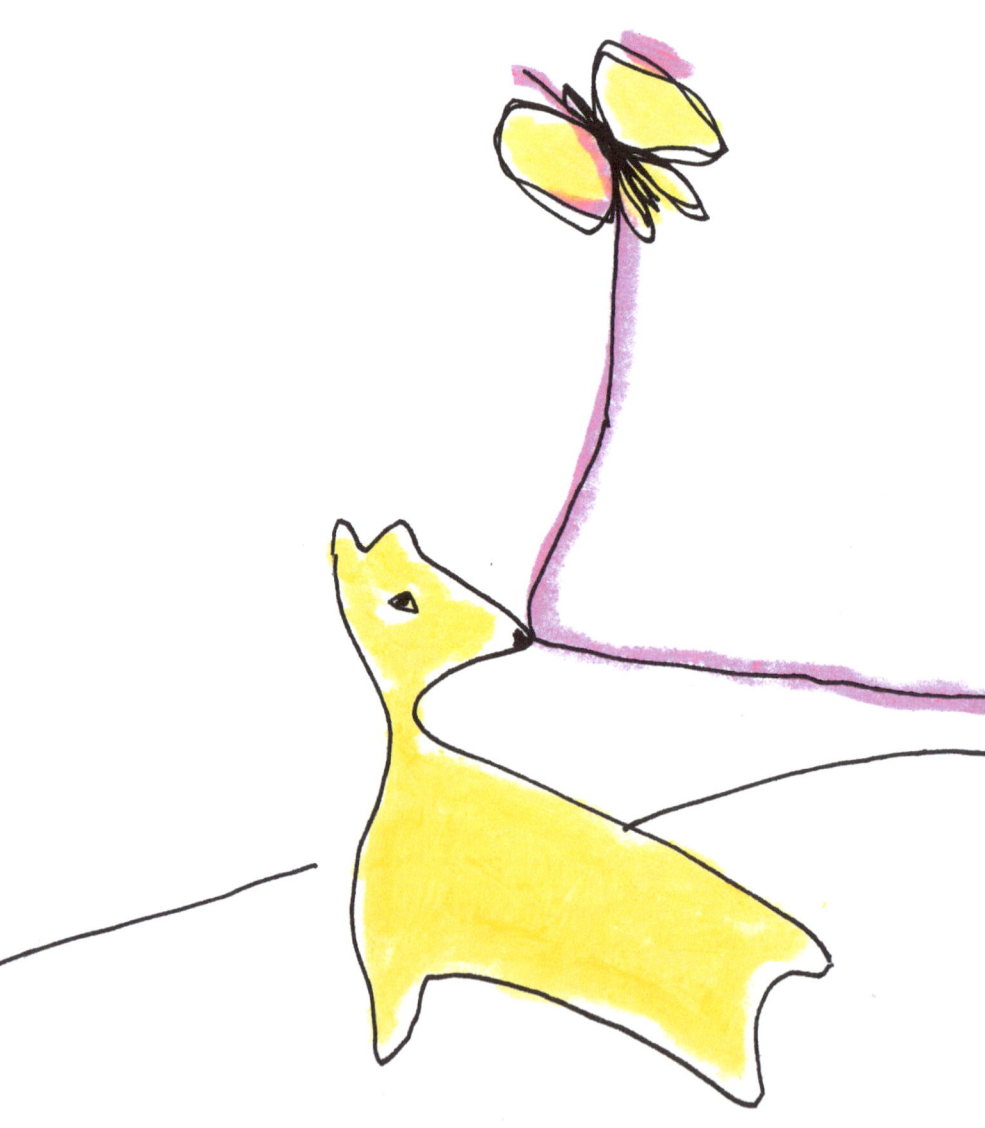

Butterfly heard of Lion's
impending doom. With the
help of Fox, Butterfly came
to see Lion.

They brought the magic
pink yarn.

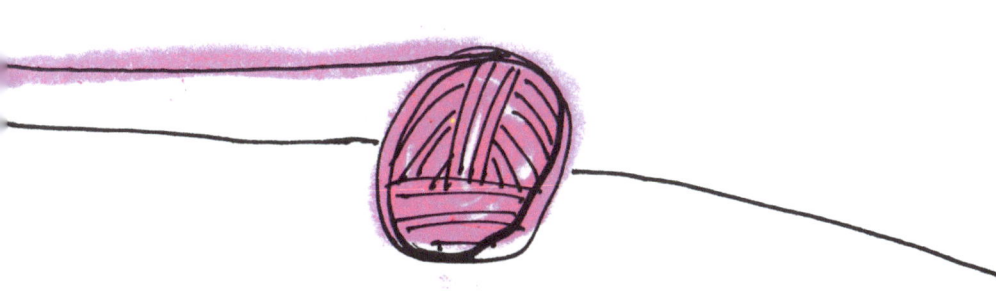

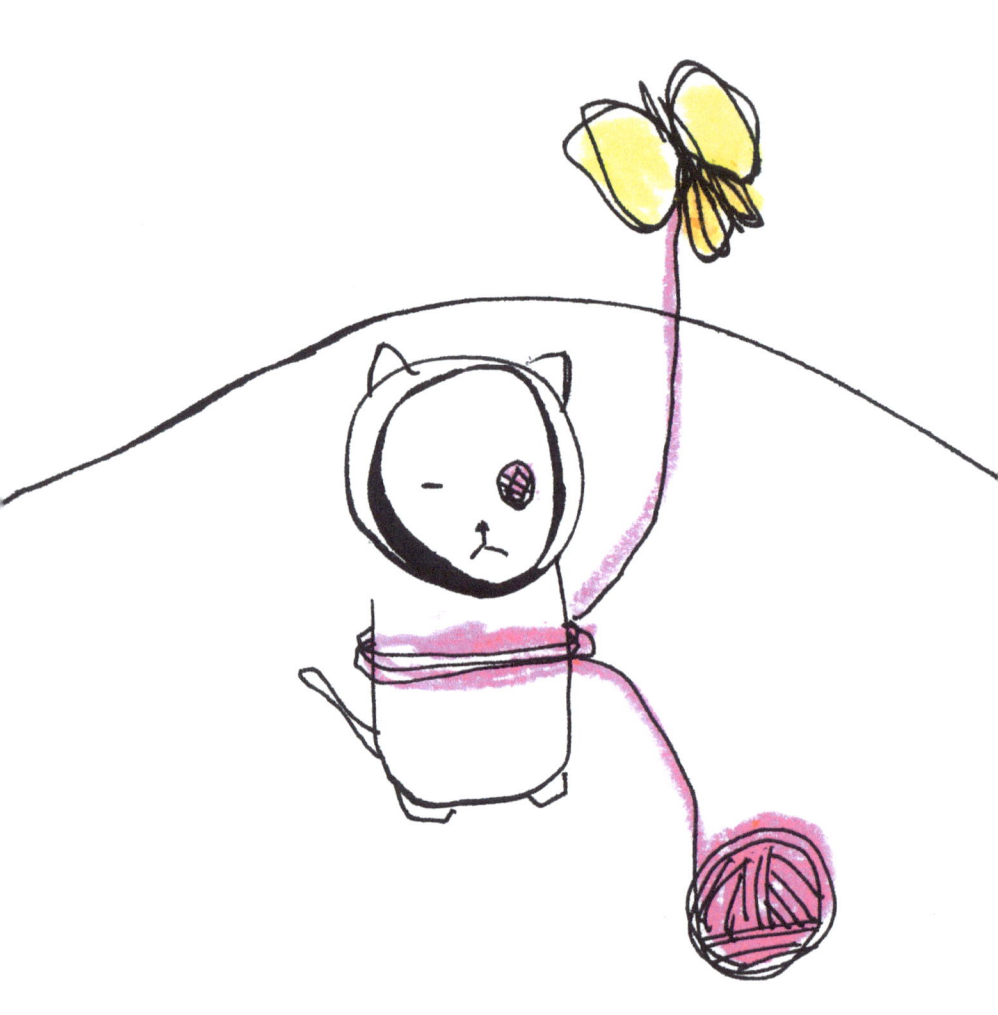

With the pink yarn,
Butterfly made an eye patch
and put it over Lion's eye.

The yarn was also wrapped
around Lion's chest, over
the wound.

meanwhile, FangGrrr picked up the
bow and arrow and went looking

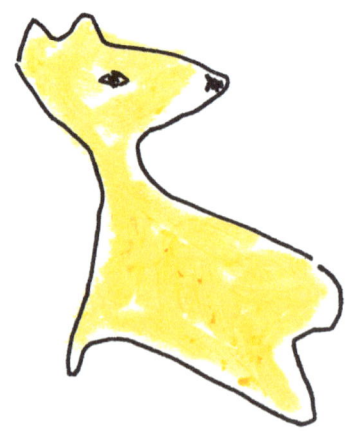

for snake.

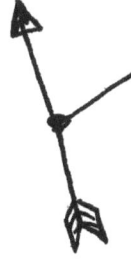

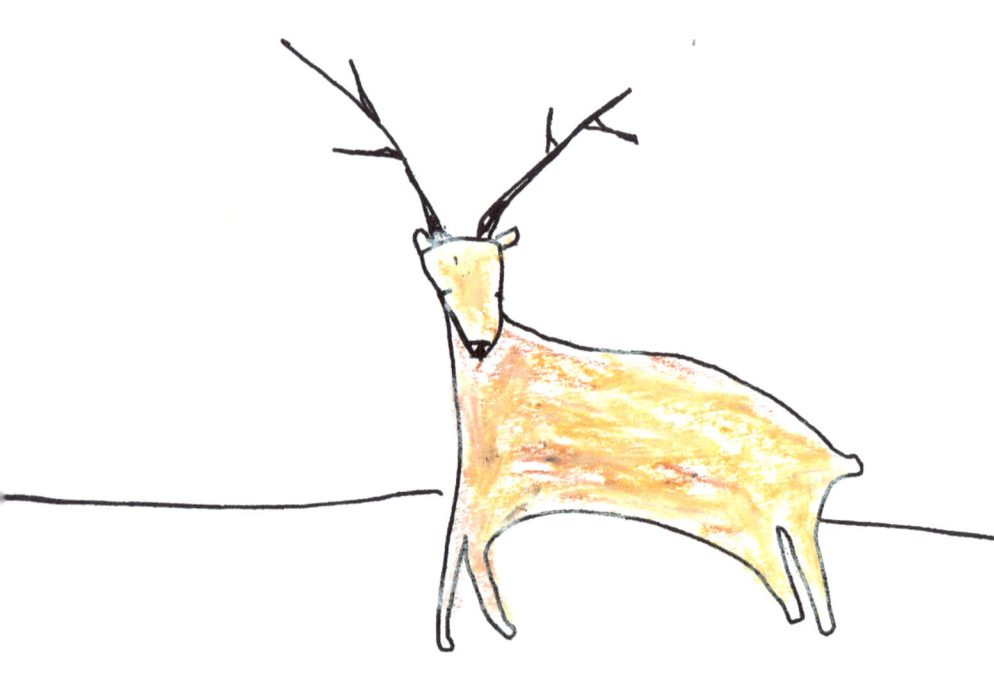

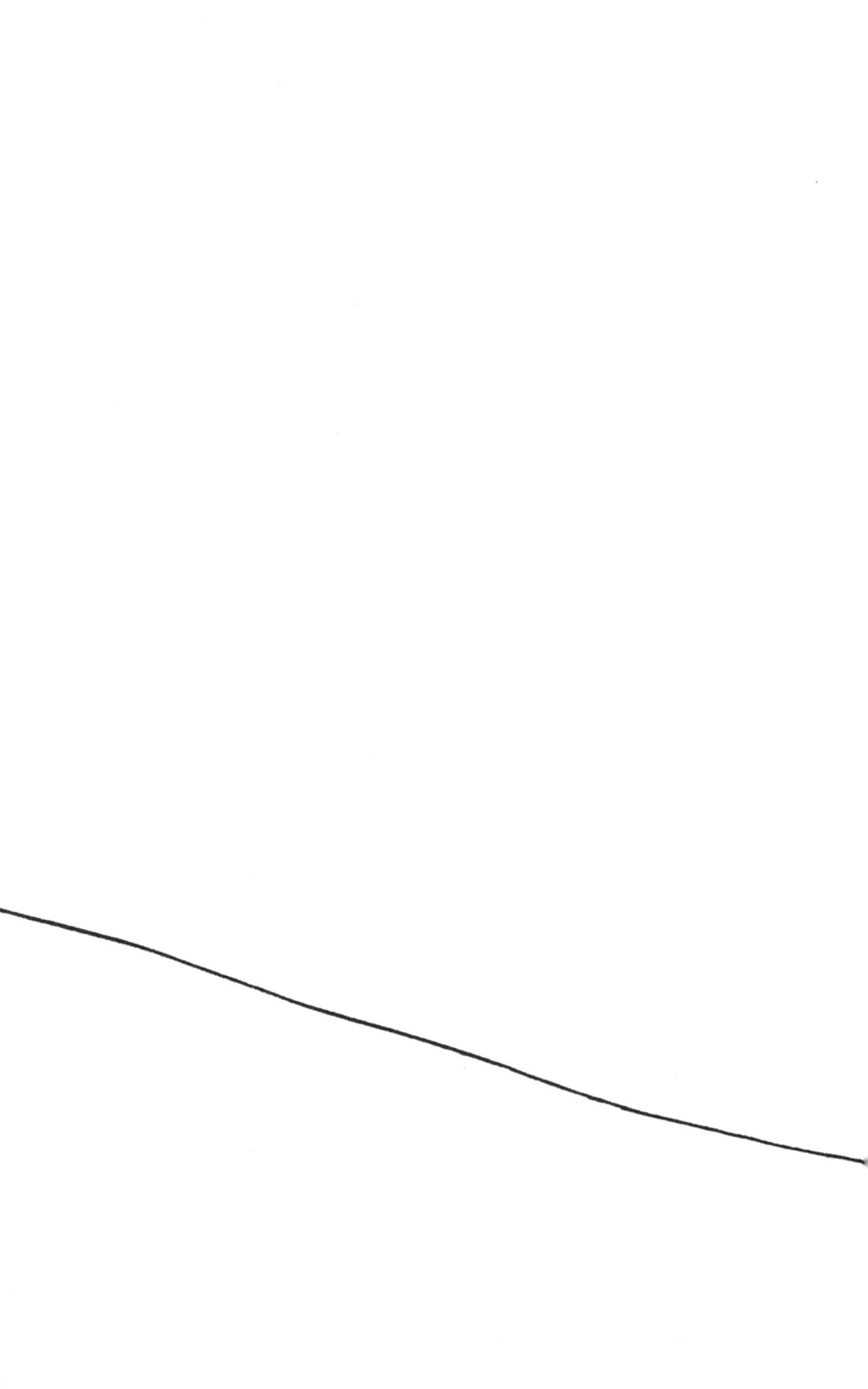

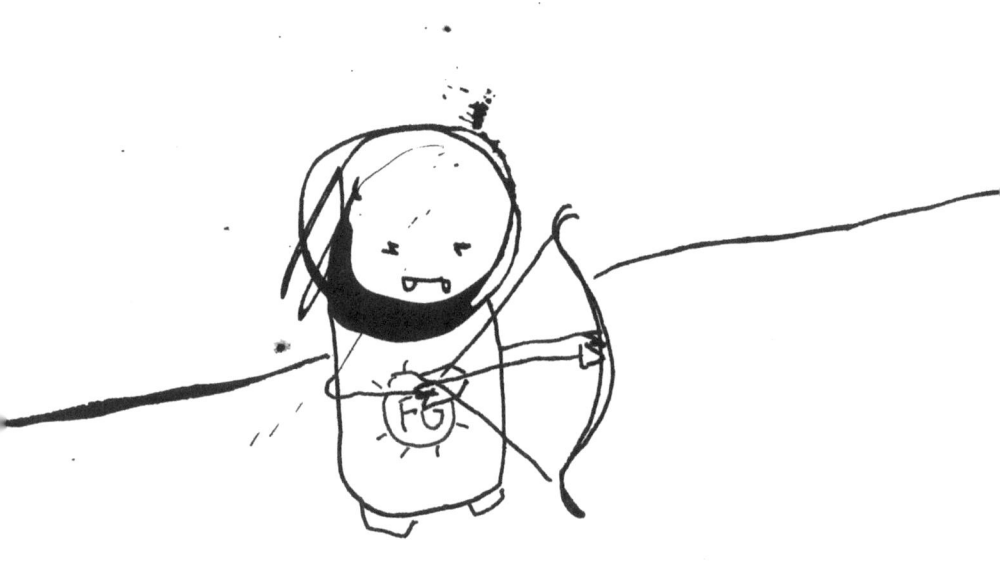

"Prepare to die," said
FangGrrr to Snake.

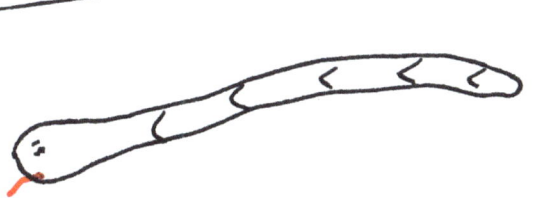

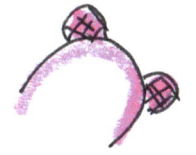

Right as FangGrrr
was about to release
the arrow, Butterfly
fluttered in and said

"Wait, FangGrrr."

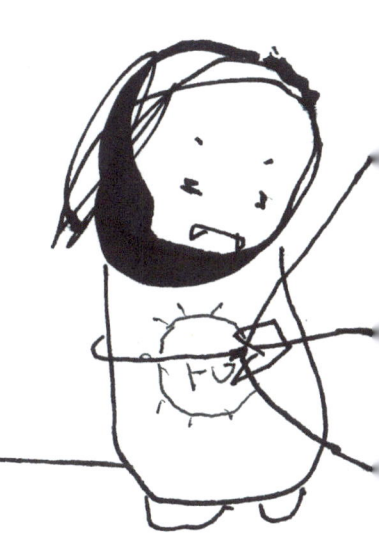

"Wait."

"Killing Snake will not kill
your pain," said Butterfly.

"But Snake told me to hurt
Lion and Lion may soon
be dead," said FangGrr.

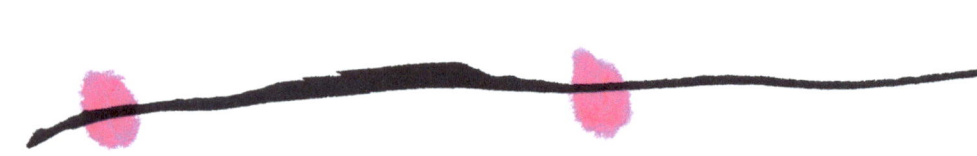

"Snake told you to hurt Lion
but _you_ are the one who hurt Lion."

"i don't know what to do. What should
i do, Butterfly?"

"That is not the question."

"Then what is?"

"The question is...

...what **WILL** you do? "

"what will you do,

FangGrrr? "

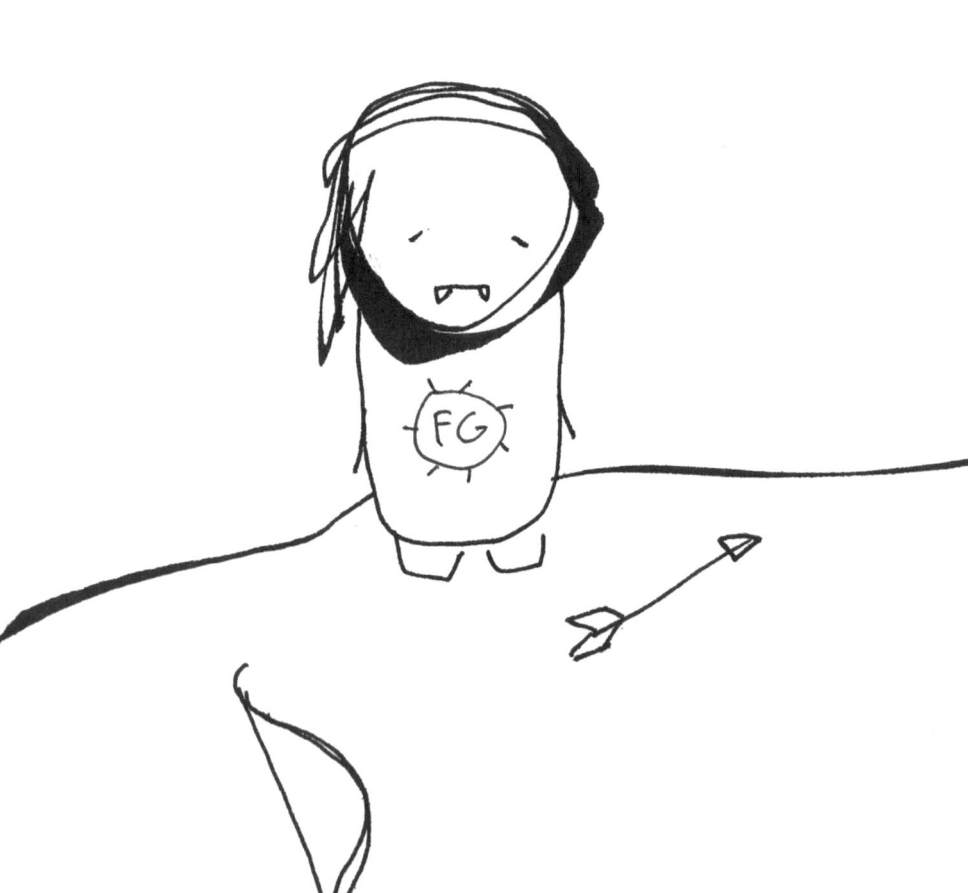

Fangburr put the bow
and arrow down.

Snake slithered away.

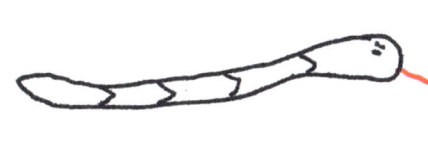

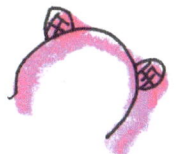

"i am wretched,"

said FangGrr.

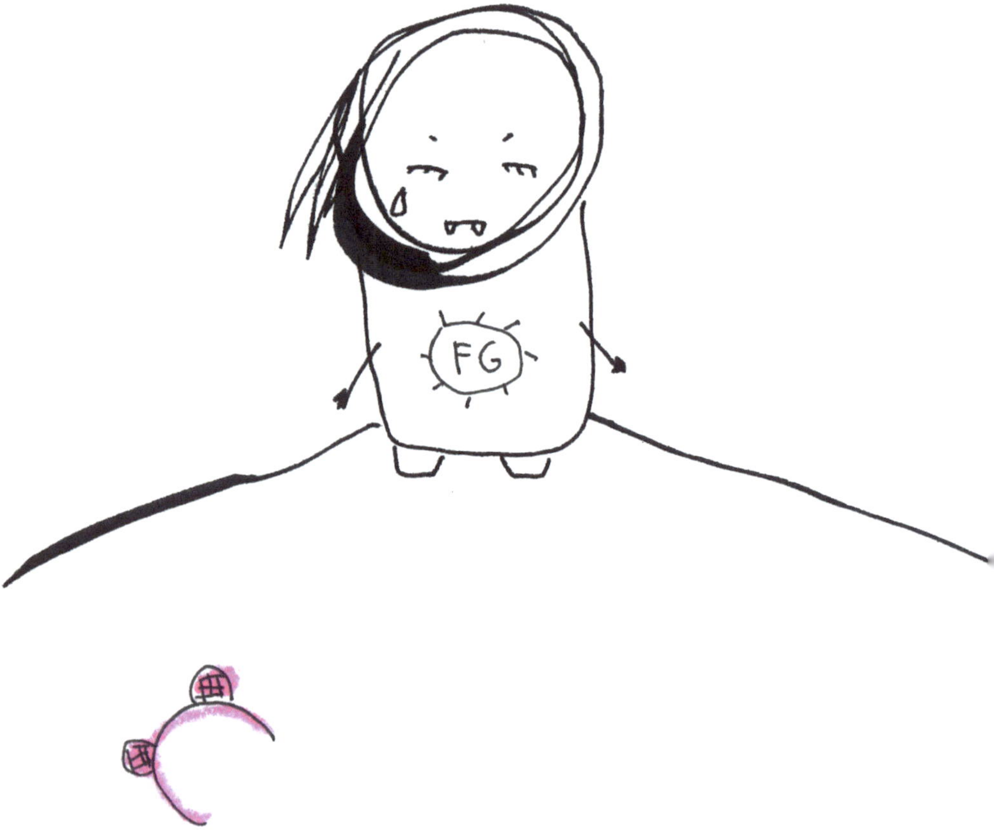

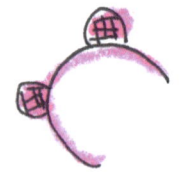

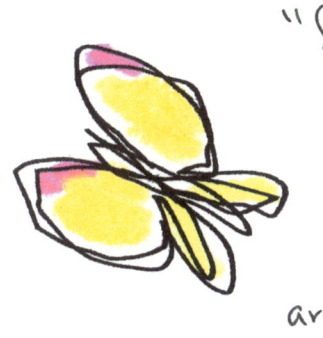

"Sometimes we are,"
said Butterfly,

"but sometimes we
are wonderful. Like now.
You could have made more hate but
you didn't. You made good."

"But actually, i'm not good. i'm bad."

"You're not good <u>or</u> bad, FangGrr.
You're good <u>and</u> bad. We all are."

"And by the way, it's not your fault that your mom and dad left you, FangGrrr," said Butterfly.

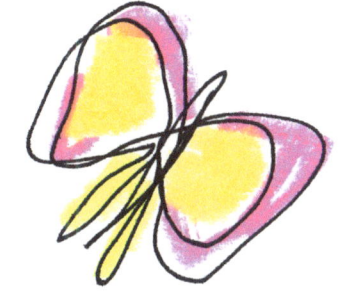

"Now let's go check
on Lion."

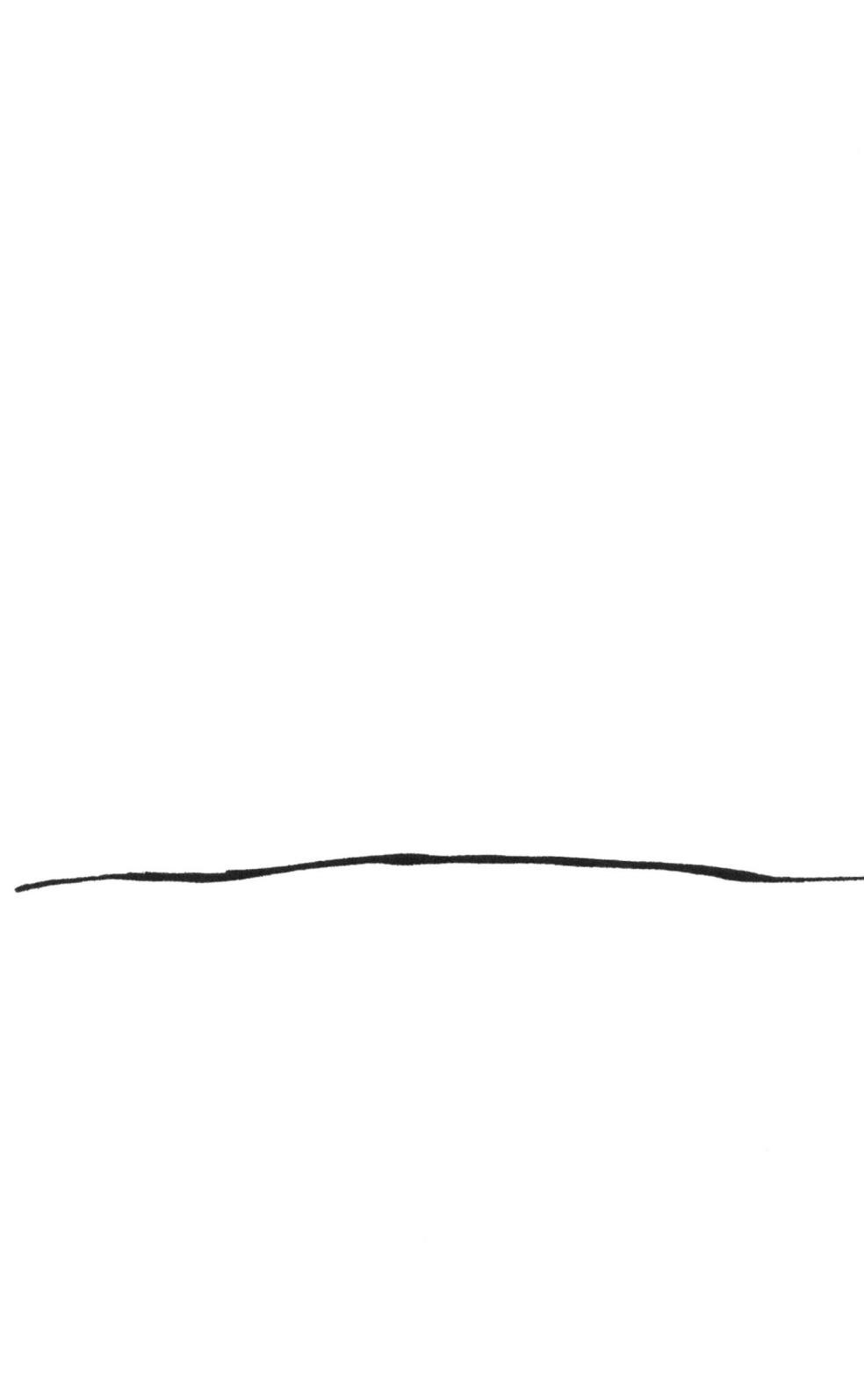

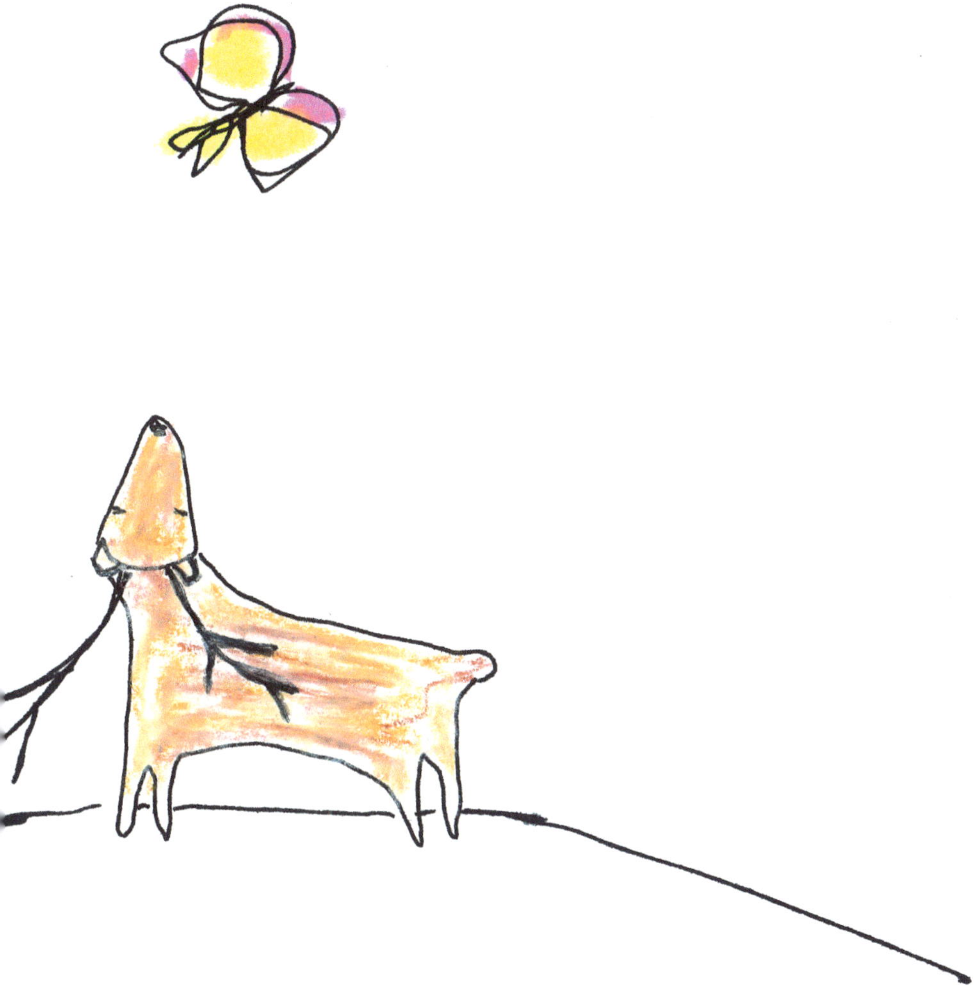

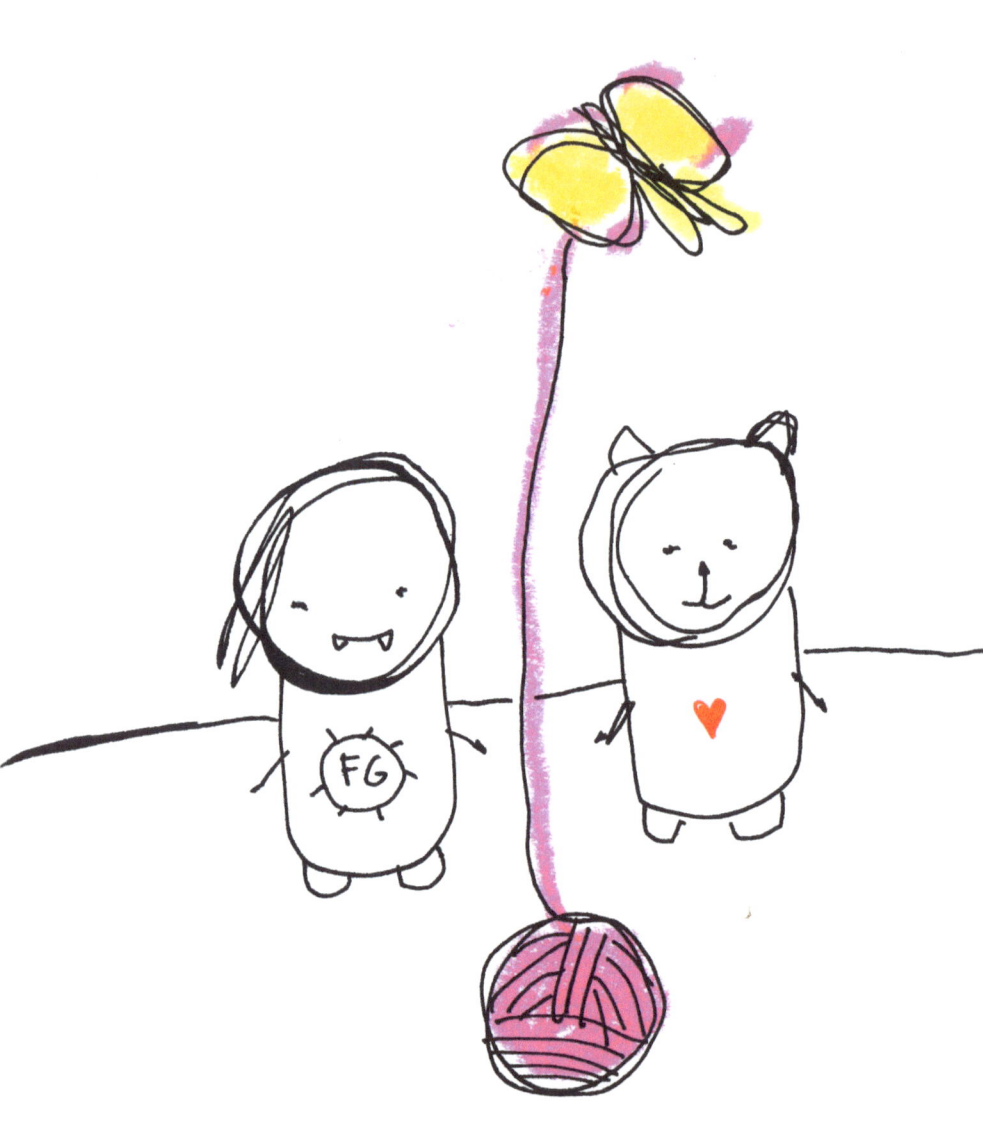

FangGrrr and Butterfly returned
to an all-better Lion. The
magic yarn had brought
Lion back from death.

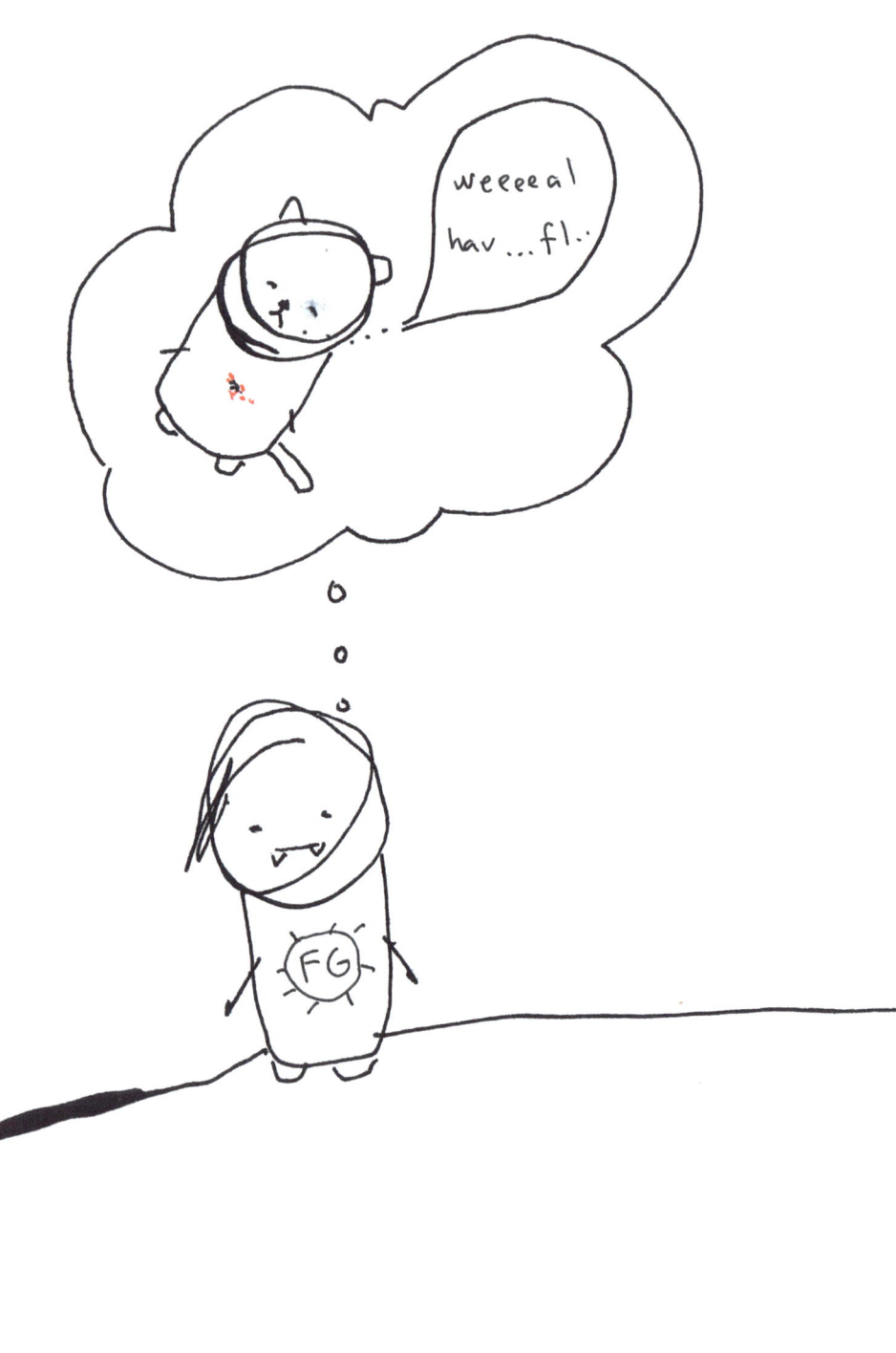

"Lion, what were you trying to say to me when you were dying?" asked FangGrrr.

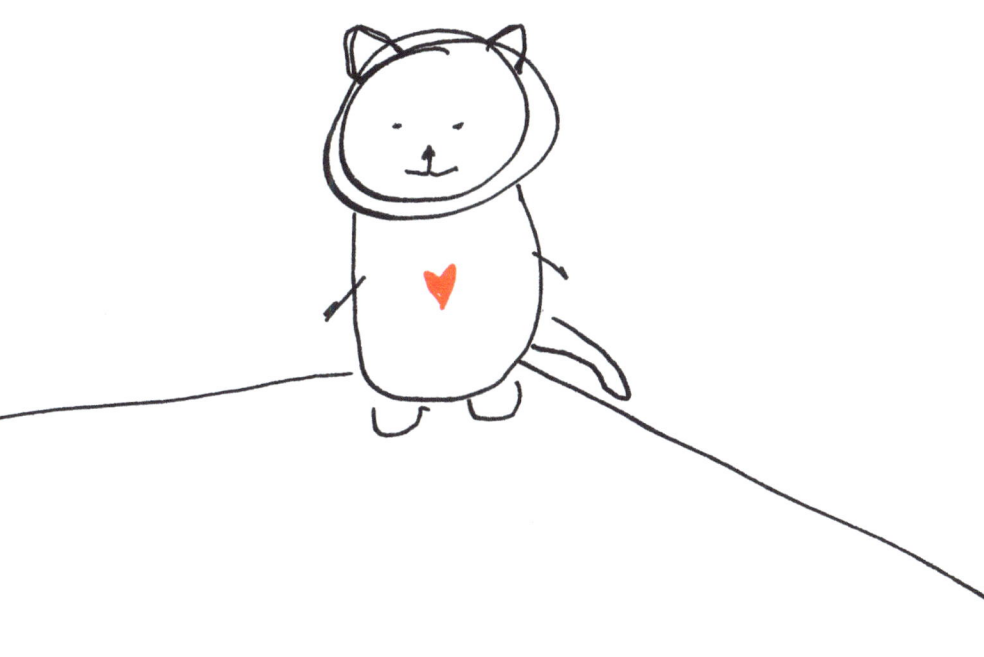

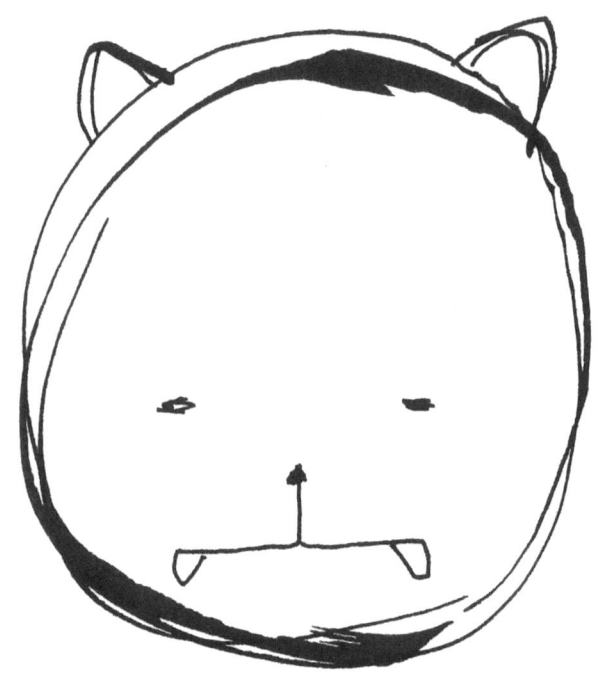

"i was trying to say that we
all have flaws and fangs, FangGurr.
i have them too, see?"

"You are not alone, FangGrr.

We all hurt."

"We all hurt AND

we all love,"

said Lion.

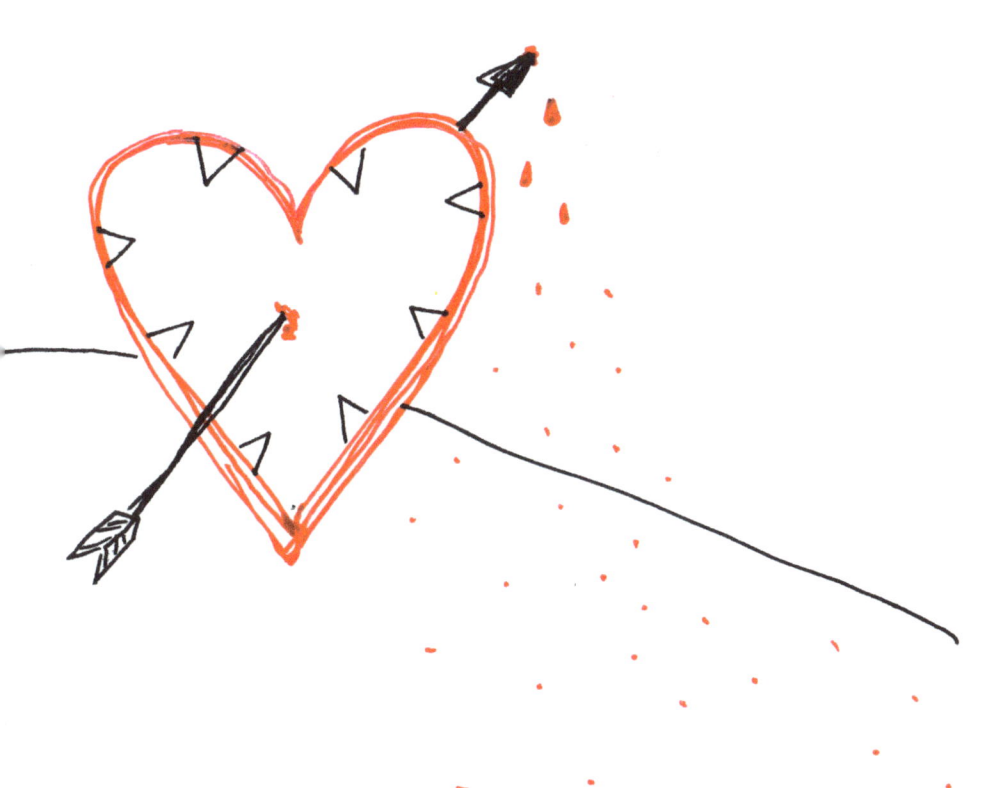

"But what about Snake?"
asked FangGrr. "He gets
off Scott-Free?"

"The more you engage with Snake
the more you empower Snake,"
said Lion.

"Snake is a hate-maker. Disengage
with hate-makers.

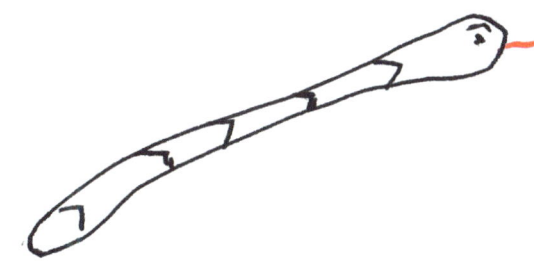

"By the way, Snake is not
free."

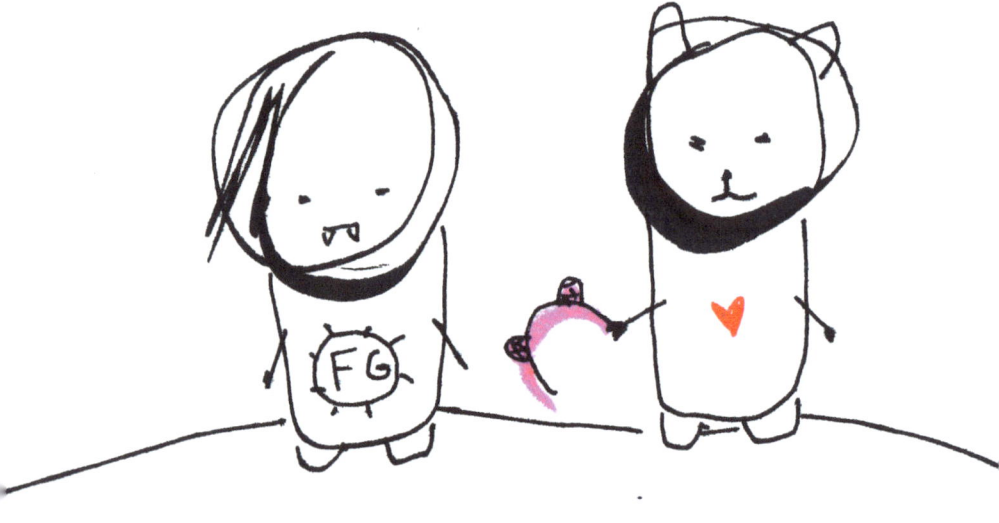

"So FangGrrr, i think you should put your ears back on. If you want to," said Lion.

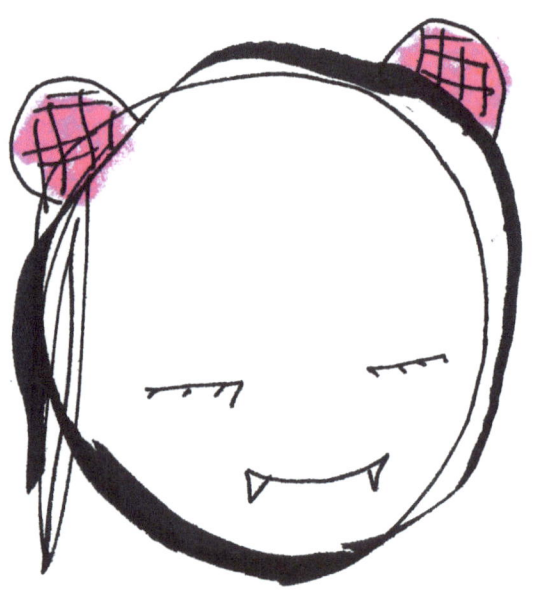

And so FangGrrr did.

Because FangGrrr wanted
to. FangGrrr was ready
to play once more.

And with that, FangGrrr, Lion, Butterfly, Fox, and other friends played.

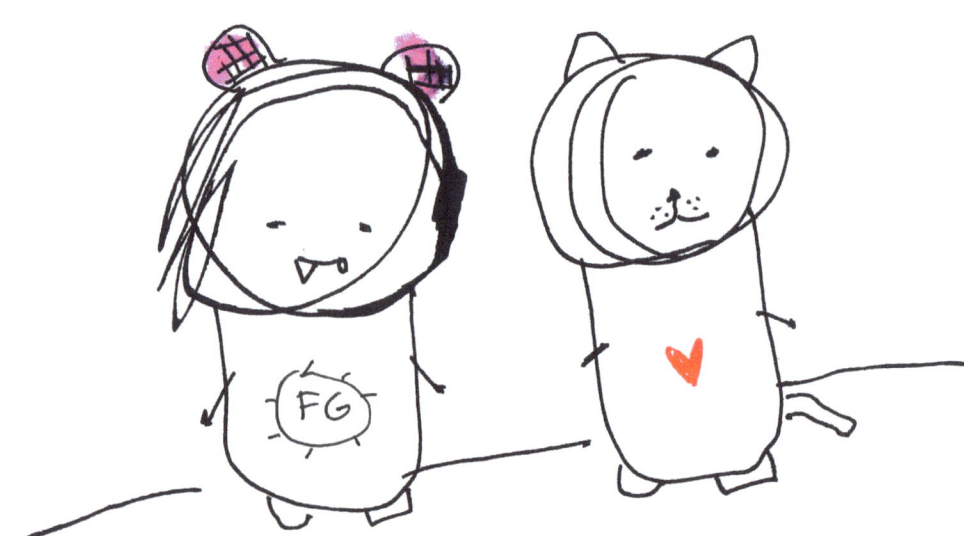

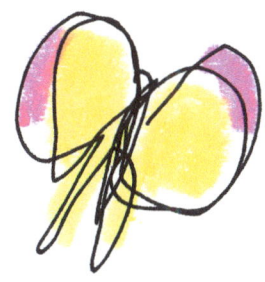

And they lived sometimes
happily AND sometimes
sorrowfully ever after.

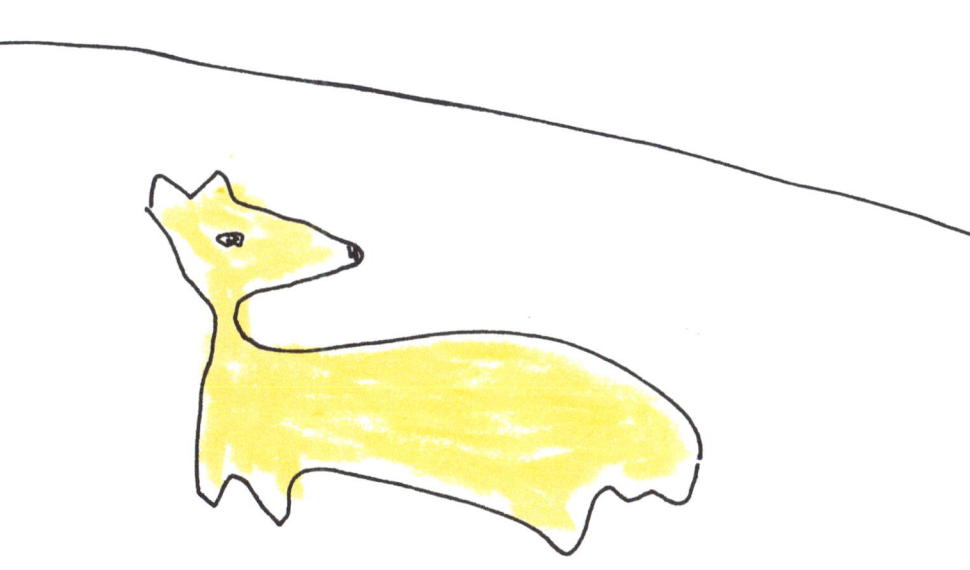

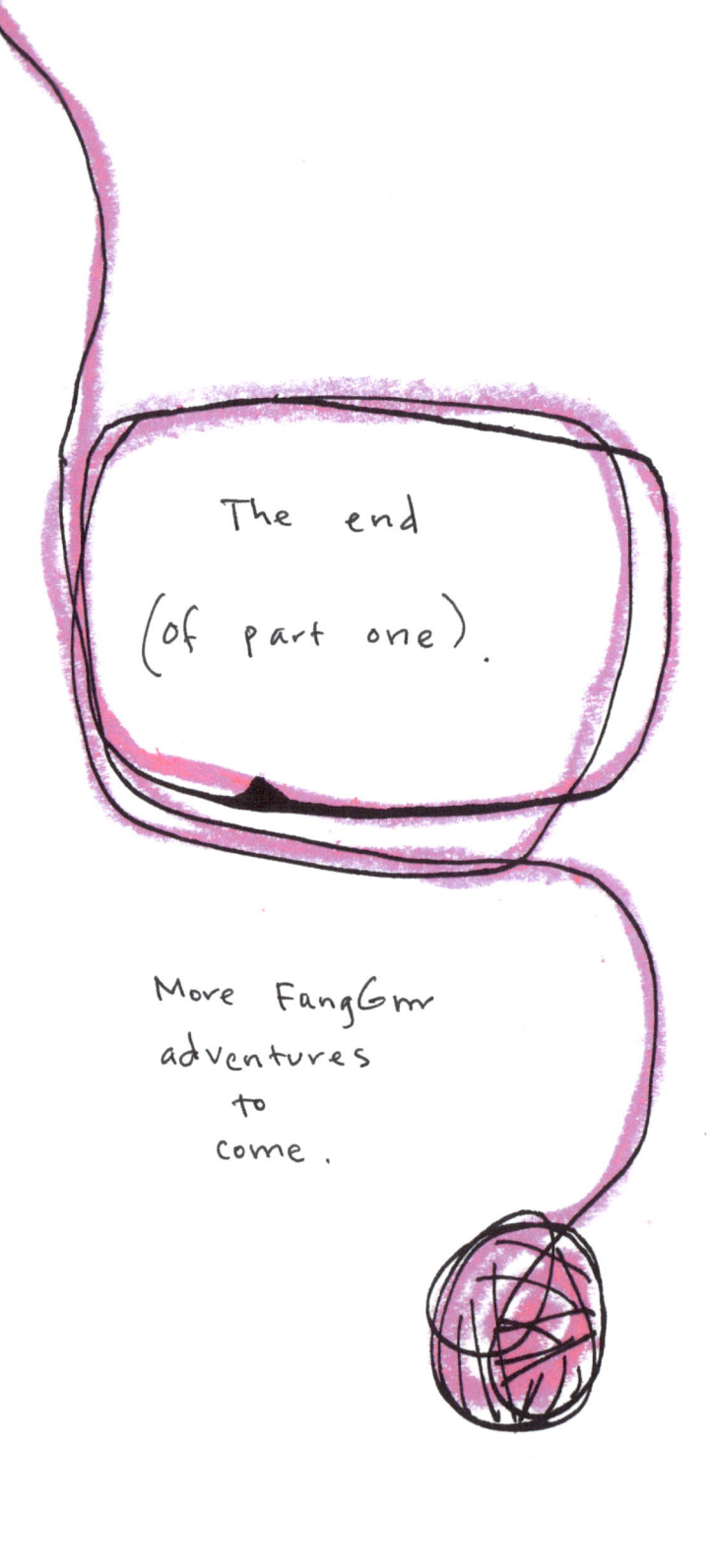

The end

(of part one).

More FangGnn
adventures
to
come.

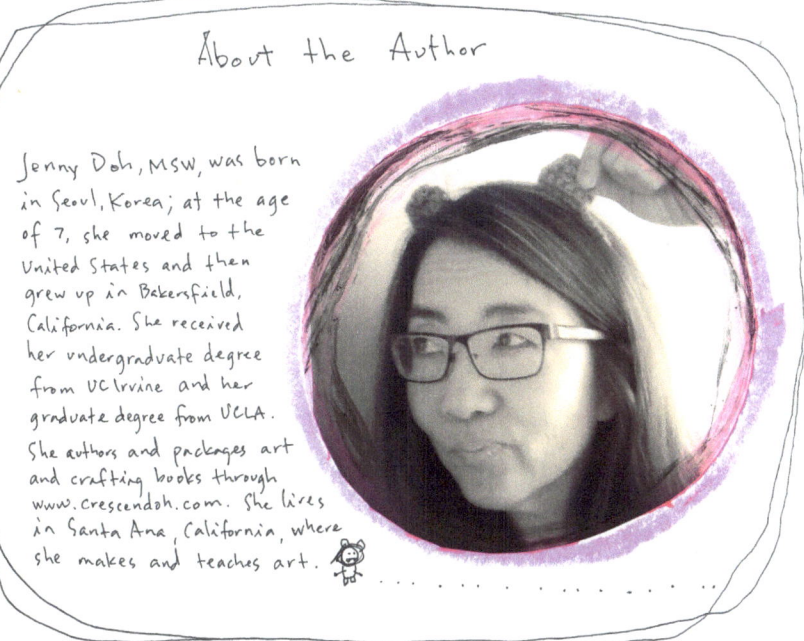

About the Author

Jenny Doh, MSW, was born in Seoul, Korea; at the age of 7, she moved to the United States and then grew up in Bakersfield, California. She received her undergraduate degree from UC Irvine and her graduate degree from UCLA.

She authors and packages art and crafting books through www.crescendoh.com. She lives in Santa Ana, California, where she makes and teaches art.

Writer and Illustrator: Jenny Doh
Copyeditor: Amanda Crabtree Weston
Designer: Raquel Joya